INQUEST

ALSO BY EDWARD JAY EPSTEIN

Counterplot

Inquest

The Warren Commission and the
Establishment of Truth

BY

Edward Jay Epstein

INTRODUCTION BY RICHARD H. ROVERE

The Viking Press • New York

Viking Compass Edition
Issued in 1969 by The Viking Press, Inc.
625 Madison Avenue, New York, N.Y. 10022

Distributed in Canada by
The Macmillan Company of Canada Limited

Library of Congress catalog card number: 66-21197

Printed in U.S.A.

CONTENTS

Illustrations

INTRODUCTION

BY RICHARD H. ROVERE

"The quest for truth in the Kennedy assassination has been long and arduous," Harrison E. Salisbury wrote in his introduction to an edition of the Warren Commission Report published under the stately imprimatur of *The New York Times*. "The Warren Commission spent the better part of a year in exhaustive investigation of every particle of evidence it could discover. . . . No material question now remains unresolved so far as the death of President Kennedy is concerned. [The] evidence of [Lee Harvey] Oswald's single-handed guilt is overwhelming."

Now, less than two years after the Warren Commission closed its books, we are confronted by a report on its report that challenges almost every one of these satisfied and admiring words, and I find it my appalling duty to state that in my

opinion the words do not withstand the challenge. Edward
Jay Epstein maintains—and, I believe, amply demonstrates—
that the "quest for truth" was also a quest for domestic tran-
quillity, that the second quest often got in the way of the first,
and that in any case the pursuit was by no means as "long and
arduous" as it should have been. Mr. Salisbury said that the
Commission spent "the better part of a year in exhaustive
investigation." Mr. Epstein shows that the investigation proper
lasted less than ten weeks, that it fell far short of being exhaustive, and that the Warren Commission as such—that is to
say, the Chief Justice of the United States and the six other
eminent Americans appointed to serve under him by the
President on November 29, 1963—played a minor and often
inattentive part in the proceedings. "No material question remains unresolved," Mr. Salisbury wrote. Mr. Epstein discloses
that at least one large question of incontestable materiality—
the number of rifle shots fired at the Presidential party—was
never resolved, not even, astonishingly, to the satisfaction of
the Commissioners themselves. He believes that the case for
Oswald's guilt was solidly established. But he insists that evidence of Oswald's "single-handed" guilt was not, as Mr. Salisbury has it, "overwhelming," but incomplete and highly vul-
nerable.

Mr. Epstein, a brilliant young academician, is not hawk-
ing any sensations or playing any hunches about a conspiracy to kill John F. Kennedy. He is not saying that there *was*
a second assassin or that proof of the existence of one would
necessarily alter the fundamental nature of the case. (If one
Oswald was possible, why not two? It would not have been
the first crime committed by a pair of "loners"—vide *In Cold
Blood* by Truman Capote.) He is dealing with the record and
disentangling the evidence from the conclusions. "If there was
no evidence of more than one assassin," he writes, "there was
also no evidence that precluded the possibility." The case for

Oswald's single-handed guilt rests, as of now, wholly on the Warren Commission's finding that only three bullets were fired at the Presidential party and that one of these described an eccentric course through the bodies of President Kennedy and Governor John Connally of Texas. According to Mr. Epstein, "There was, however, no substantial evidence which supported this contention, and there was evidence that all but precluded the possibility that both men had been hit by the same bullet." I will not attempt here to restate or condense Mr. Epstein's line of reasoning. He makes his own case adroitly and with an economy of language I might find myself unable to match. That the case is as impressive as it is disturbing is borne out, in my view, by the fact—brought to light here for the first time—that the Warren Commission was itself divided on this crucial matter and that it settled the question by what some members called "the battle of the adjectives." In characterizing the evidence on which its single most important conclusion rests, the strongest word the Commissioners could agree upon was "persuasive." A word they could not agree upon was "compelling."

Mr. Epstein does not challenge or even question the fundamental integrity of the Commission or its staff. He discards as shabby "demonology" the view that the Commissioners collusively suppressed evidence. He pays the Commission Report the high compliment of close scrutiny. His concern when he undertook this study was not with the conclusions the Commission reached; it was with the processes of fact-finding employed by an agency having a complex and in some ways ambiguous relationship to the bureaucracy that brought it into being. "The primary subject of this book is the Warren Commission, not the assassination," he says. And although, along the way, he raises some sharp questions about the assassination, he adheres rigorously to his fundamental purpose: an examination of the way in which a group of Americans prominent in public and professional life carried out an assignment given them by their President, that assignment being, in the language of Executive Order 11130, "to ascertain, evaluate, and report upon the facts relating to the assassination of the late President John F. Kennedy."

Executive Order 11130 was promulgated by a President seven days in office and at a moment in history when the merest show of presence of mind seemed a triumph over the environment. If some of us may now find ourselves critical, it is thanks to hindsight and to the kind of insight this book provides. As Mr. Epstein says, the President could find little guidance in American history. Mr. Epstein believes that the closest thing to a precedent for the Warren Commission was the Roberts Commission that prepared a report on the Japanese attack on Pearl Harbor. This is probably so, although it occurs to me that some procedures might have been borrowed from government regulatory agencies—for example, the Federal Aviation Agency in its disinterested and meticulous investigations of airplane accidents. But even to suggest such comparisons is to show how incomparable a situation President Johnson faced in his first days in office. In any event, if Mr. Epstein's analysis is as generally sound as I believe it to be, one of the major failings of the Warren Commission arose from the concept of expertise which was in the President's mind when he chose the members and in the members' minds when they chose their staff. The seven Commissioners were chosen more for their known probity than for their mastery of probative techniques. And the Commissioners, lawyers without exception, hired a staff of lawyers. These were chosen as much for their professional standing as for the skills and experience relevant to the problem at hand. The Commissioners evidently gave some thought to hiring men with other skills and backgrounds but did not do so because they felt that they could call on all sorts of experts already in federal employment. "Because of the diligence, cooperation, and facilities of Federal investigative agencies," they said in their own foreword to the Report, "it was unnecessary for the Commissioners to employ investigators other than members of the Commission's legal staff."

The Commission, then, was a committee of lawyers, all of whom were also public servants and men with present or very recent connections with the federal government. It was assisted almost exclusively by lawyers. Lawyers serve clients as doctors serve patients and teachers serve students. Technically, the Commission's client was Lyndon B. Johnson; its official title was the President's Commission on the Assassination of President John F. Kennedy. All that the President asked of the Commission was the truth, and truth was what the Commissioners sought. But at crucial points the Commission's structure, its procedures, and, finally, the peculiar atmosphere in which it worked hampered and deflected its search. Its professional investigative arm was the Federal Bureau of Investigation, in many ways an estimable organization but one with interests of its own to protect. Thus, when the question arose as to whether Lee Harvey Oswald had ever been an informant for the FBI, the Commission sought an answer from the FBI and was assured that it had never employed Oswald. The answer may have been the truth and nothing but the truth. One may be certain, though, that the answer would have been No even if it should have been Yes.

The Commission, however, might still have been skeptical of the answer if it had not itself a rather similar interest to serve. It did not, after all, accept *all* the FBI's findings on the assassination, as Mr. Epstein points out and as a reading of FBI reports, excerpts of which are published here as appendices, will demonstrate. If the FBI had its own bureaucratic prestige to maintain, the Commission, being what it was and doing what it was doing, had the prestige of the entire United

States to think about. Its client of record was the President, but to serve the President of the United States is to serve not a man but a government, a nation, a great sovereignty. This creates a problem. I could not hope to state it better than Mr. Epstein does:

> There was thus a dualism in purpose. If the explicit purpose of the Commission was to ascertain and expose the facts, the implicit purpose was to protect the national interest by dispelling rumors.
>
> These two purposes were compatible so long as the damaging rumors were untrue. But what if a rumor damaging to the national interest proved to be true? The Commission's explicit purpose would dictate that the information be exposed regardless of the consequences, while the Commission's implicit purpose would dictate that the rumor be dispelled regardless of the fact that it was true. In a conflict of this sort, one of the Commission's purposes would emerge as dominant.

And there were other conflicts. The President chose widely known men for the Commission. Such men are generally very busy men. The Chief Justice and leaders of Congress have fixed responsibilities they can neglect only at high public cost. They were part-time investigators of the assassination, thus leaving themselves open to charges of serving as "front men." By Mr. Epstein's account, a "front" is a fairly accurate description of the Commission. Behind it was the staff. But it was made up not merely of competent lawyers but of highly successful ones who, like the Commissioners, had other institutions and interests to serve. Nothing Mr. Epstein reveals is quite so shocking as the fact that this great investigation was carried out by men who could not give their full attention to it and who, because of their own needs and also because of certain political circumstances, were in a desperate hurry to get it over with.

When I first read Mr. Epstein's book it was with the hope that I would find it greatly flawed and could advise that it was not a work to be taken seriously. In late 1963 and in 1964 I was one with what I am sure was a majority of Americans in that the theory of the assassination that best suited me was the one that the Warren Commission in time said best suited the facts. I accepted its Report and was pleased, or at least relieved, to discover that most of the published attacks on it were transparently malicious or ignorant. I would not have been altogether displeased to be able to say the same of Mr. Epstein's book. But I found it from start to finish responsible, sober, and, to use the word the Commission could not bring itself to use, compelling. It is a public service of the kind one wishes were unnecessary. But this does not diminish its importance or its value. And what is perhaps most valuable and important about it is that it may help make future public services of its kind unnecessary.

Finally, as a journalist, I should like to point out that Mr. Epstein's book is the work of a scholar and very much a product of the academy. Nowadays in my profession and elsewhere it is fashionable to deplore academic research, except in the natural sciences, and, from what I have seen, much of it is deplorable. But here we have something which should make scholars proud and journalists envious and ashamed. The day the Warren Commission Report was issued, the American press should have begun to do what Mr. Epstein has done; it should have cast a very cool eye on the Report and sought to learn from those who prepared it how it was prepared, who did the heavy work, and what individual workers thought of the collective product. Mr. Epstein's scholarly tools happen to be those employed day in and day out by journalists. But the press left it to a single scholar to find the news.

PREFACE

ONE WEEK after President John F. Kennedy was assassinated, President Lyndon B. Johnson appointed a Commission, headed by Chief Justice Earl Warren, to ascertain the facts concerning the assassination. The Commission, generally known as the Warren Commission, reported its findings ten months later.

The primary subject of this book is the Warren Commission, not the assassination itself. It attempts to answer the question: How did the Commission go about searching for such an elusive and many-faced quarry as the truth?

There have been many Presidential commissions in the past. Most of them have been concerned with gathering information on a given subject, which is something quite different from seeking *the* truth. Few of these commissions have had either the power to compel testimony or the mandate to conduct a penetrating investigation.[1]* Perhaps the closest parallel to the Warren Commission was the Roberts Commission, which investigated the Japanese attack on Pearl Harbor. However, the Roberts Commission was essentially a military commission. With the exception of Supreme Court Justice Owen J. Roberts, all its members were admirals and generals, and the commission was primarily interested in the problem of evaluating military preparedness.[2]

The Warren Commission faced an entirely different sort of problem: it had to find the solution to a very complex and involved mystery. Witnesses had to be questioned, evidence had to be verified, hypotheses had to be tested, clues had to be pursued. In short, the Commission had to conduct an exhaustive investigation, evaluate and weigh all the facts, and arrive at an answer.

This study deals with four central questions arising out of the Commission's work. The first question is: How did the Commission, under virtually unprecedented circumstances, initiate, organize, and direct a full-scale investigation?

Second, there is the more general problem of truth-finding in a political environment. Unlike scientific or philosophical investigations, in which the pursuit of truth can be insulated from external circumstances, a governmental inquiry does not take place in a vacuum. When Arthur Sylvester, Assistant Secretary of Defense for Public Affairs, said in 1962 that a government has an inherent right to lie to save itself, he was referring to a missile crisis that directly threatened the national interest.[3] Such political truth is expected in time of war— or when war is imminent—but there are other situations in which the national interest is less easily defined. The Warren Commission was involved in just such a situation; the nation's

* Notes will be found beginning on p. 205.

faith in its own institutions was held to be at stake. It is thus important to consider to what degree, if at all, this consideration affected the truth-finding process of the Warren Commission.

Third, there is the problem of the investigation itself. What was the scope and depth of the investigation, and what were its limits?

Finally, there is the question of how the Commission's Report was written. From the mass of accumulated facts, some had to be included, others omitted. To understand the Report, it is necessary to understand the process by which evidence was selected.

These four problems are the main concern of this study. Even if these questions could be fully answered, a complete picture of the Commission would probably not emerge. The answers might, however, give some insight into the nature of the Commission.

With regard to the Commission, most of the writing on the assassination to date falls into two diametrically opposed categories: demonology and blind faith.[4] Writers in both groups seem to subscribe to an assumption of governmental omnipotence—i.e., that the government can do whatever it sets out to do. Thus the demonologists reason that as all the facts were not revealed, the Warren Commission must have been party to a conspiracy to suppress evidence. The blindly faithful reason that as the Warren Commission would not be party to a conspiracy, all the pertinent evidence must therefore be known. It should be noted that this study rejects both lines of reasoning because it rejects the common assumption on which they are based.

The research for this study was based on four main sources. The first source is the Commission's Report[5] and the twenty-six volumes of testimony and exhibits upon which the Report is based.[6]

The second source is the investigative reports in the United States National Archives. Although a portion of the material is not yet declassified, most of the pertinent investigative reports were unclassified and available for this study.[7]

The third source is the working papers of the Commission supplied by a member of the staff. This material, and especially his chronological file, were of particular importance in understanding the mechanics of the Commission.[8]

The fourth, and most important, source was the interviews conducted for this study between March 23, 1965, and September 29, 1965. Among those interviewed were five of the seven members of the Commission: Senator John Sherman Cooper,[9] Representative Hale Boggs,[10] Representative Gerald R. Ford,[11] Allen W. Dulles,[12] and John J. McCloy.[13] Also interviewed were J. Lee Rankin, the Commission's General Counsel;[14] Norman Redlich, Rankin's special assistant;[15] Howard P. Willens, the administrative assistant;[16] and Alfred Goldberg, who, together with Redlich, had editorial responsibility for writing the Report.[17]

Six of the assistant counsel who conducted the investigation were also interviewed: Francis W. H. Adams,[18] Joseph A. Ball,[19] Melvin A. Eisenberg,[20] Wesley J. Liebeler,[21] Arlen Specter,[22] and Samuel A. Stern.[23]

This book began as a master's thesis in government at Cornell University. The initial stimulus was a problem posed by Professor Andrew Hacker: How does a government organization function in an extraordinary situation in which there are no rules or precedents to guide it? Needless to say, when I selected the Warren Commission for a case study, I thought the problem far less complicated and intriguing than it proved to be.

I am deeply grateful to Lois and Andrew Hacker for the assistance, criticism, and time they gave me. Without their encouragement and understanding this book would never have been finished. I would also like to thank Alan A. Altshuler, David E. Green, Jones Harris, Sylvia Meagher, and Toni Mergentime for reading the manuscript and making many valuable suggestions. Finally, I wish to thank Arnold R. Krakower for giving me a legal perspective on the problems of the Commission.

—EDWARD JAY EPSTEIN

Cambridge, Massachusetts
March 1966

It is not altogether clear whether the controversy over the validity of the Warren Report that has arisen in the last three years has produced more heat than light. Literally hundreds of hypotheses about the assassination, some more preposterous than others, have been proposed, and the district attorney of New Orleans, Jim Garrison, acting out his theories in what might be called a living theater, has actually arrested a number of individuals on conspiracy charges. On the other hand, serious attempts have been made to lessen the confusion over the evidence. In a four-part inquiry, CBS News went a good deal further than the Warren Commission did in analyzing the sequence of the rifle shots; and although this analysis generally supported the conclusions of the Commission, it did raise some new, and important, questions about exactly when the first shot was fired. (The text of this CBS study is contained in Stephen White's book, *Should We Now Believe the Warren Report?*) Josiah Thompson, Jr., an assistant professor of philosophy at Haverford College, also went beyond the Warren Commission in examining the amateur film of the assassination, and his book, *Six Seconds in Dallas,* brings up fresh problems relating to the direction of the shots. In separate articles, Doctors Milton Helpern and Cyril Wecht, two leading forensic pathologists, have re-examined testimony and documents, finding serious omissions that cast doubt on the Commission's conclusions derived from the results of President Kennedy's autopsy.

A number of documents have also been made public since I wrote my thesis. The FBI Summary and Supplemental Reports, which were given to me by a lawyer on the Commission and published as appendices in this book, were subsequently released by the National Archives. The report of the FBI agents who attended the autopsy is now also available. It is fully consistent with the Summary and Supplemental Reports. Moreover, most of the internal records of the Commission, including the payroll and minutes of the executive meetings, have now been declassified.

This new evidence does not affect my principal conclusions about the limits of the Warren Commission's investigation. Furthermore, the crucial question about the autopsy remains at this time still unresolved. It is now known that the remains at this time still not fully resolved. It is now known that the Commission agreed at its executive meeting of April 30, 1964, to have one of its members examine, with the assistance of a doctor, the autopsy photographs and X-rays held by the Kennedy family. This was not, however, done. In 1966, the autopsy material was deposited in the National Archives by the Kennedys under the condition that it not be examined by any individual for five years, and thereafter only by persons professionally qualified to evaluate such evidence. In February 1968, at the request of Dr. Thornton Boswell, one of the physicians who performed the original autopsy, the photographs and X-rays were secretly examined by a panel of four medical experts. Their report—released in January 1969, just as this edition of *Inquest* was going to press—affirmed the Warren Commission's conclusion that the President was struck by two bullets from behind. Although some questions about the autopsy will no doubt persist until the material becomes available for independent evaluation in 1971, it seems that now, more than four years after the Warren Report was published, concrete evidence is emerging that may finally determine the exact location of the President's wounds.

—EDWARD JAY EPSTEIN

Cambridge, Massachusetts
January 1969

INQUEST

1

Overview:

THE TEN-MONTH INVESTIGATION

November

ON NOVEMBER 22, 1963, President John F. Kennedy was assassinated in Dallas, Texas. The burst of shots came at 12:30 p.m. as the Presidential motorcade slowly passed through downtown Dallas. The President was shot twice and fatally wounded. Governor John B. Connally of Texas, seated directly in front of the President, was also wounded. The President was immediately rushed to Parkland Hospital where, despite desperate efforts to prolong his life, he died at 1 p.m.

Less than one hour later Lee Harvey Oswald was arrested in connection with the murder of Dallas policeman J. D. Tippit. Oswald, a twenty-four-year-old ex-Marine who had once defected to the Soviet Union and who worked in the building from which the shots were believed to have come, was immediately suspected of being the assassin. Early the next morning he was formally charged with having assassinated the President. For almost two days, through more than twelve hours of interrogation, Oswald maintained that he was completely innocent. Then, on the morning of November 24, he himself was fatally shot in the basement of the Dallas city jail by Jack Ruby, a Dallas nightclub-owner.

On November 25, after "a conference with the White House," Texas Attorney General Waggoner Carr announced that a court of inquiry would be held by the State of Texas "to develop fully and disclose openly" the facts of the assassination. This investigation was intended to be part of a broader inquiry in which the FBI would first conduct a full investigation and report its findings to the President; then the Texas court of inquiry would examine witnesses of the assassination in public hearings; and finally a Presidential Commission would evaluate all the facts that were established and report its conclusions to the President. Waggoner Carr named two prominent Texas lawyers, Leon Jaworski and Dean Robert G. Storey, as special counsel for the investigation.[1]

On November 26 Senator Everett M. Dirksen proposed that the Senate Judiciary Committee conduct a full investigation into the assassination. This suggestion received considerable support from both Democrats and Republicans on the floor of the Senate. The next day Congressman Charles E. Goodell proposed in the House of Representatives that a Joint Committee, composed of seven Senators and seven Representatives, conduct an inquiry into the assassination.

On November 29, "to avoid parallel investigations and to concentrate fact-finding in a body having the broadest national mandate,"[2] President Lyndon B. Johnson appointed a commission "to ascertain, evaluate, and report on" the facts of the assassination.[3] Earl Warren, the Chief Justice of the United

States, was chosen as chairman, and from its inception the commission was generally known as the "Warren Commission."

To complete the Commission, President Johnson chose six men who had distinguished themselves in public life and who represented important and diverse elements in the political spectrum. Two were senior Senators: Richard B. Russell, Democrat of Georgia, who had held his seat in the Senate for thirty uninterrupted years; and John Sherman Cooper, Republican of Kentucky, who had formerly served as Ambassador to India and who was generally regarded as a leading member of the liberal wing of the Republican Party. Two were leaders of the House of Representatives: Hale Boggs, Democrat of Louisiana, Majority Whip of the House; and Gerald R. Ford, Republican of Michigan, chairman of the House Republican Conference. Two members were international lawyers: Allen W. Dulles, the former director of the Central Intelligence Agency; and John J. McCloy, former United States High Commissioner for Germany and former President of the World Bank.

The Commission was empowered to prescribe its own procedures and to employ such assistance as it deemed necessary. All government agencies were ordered to cooperate. There were few, if any, precedents in American history for such a Commission.

December

The First Meeting. On December 5, 1963, just thirteen days after the assassination of President Kennedy, the Warren Commission held its first meeting.[4] The Chief Justice presided. Allen Dulles later said, "Although we faced a difficult and perhaps unprecedented task, each of us had had a lifetime's experience in dealing with extraordinary problems, and we knew what had to be done."[5] Viewing the executive order which had created the Commission as an "unequivocal Presidential mandate" to conduct an independent investigation, the Commission decided that "the public interest in insuring that the truth was ascertained could not be met by merely accepting the reports or the analyses of Federal or State agencies."[6] All the members agreed that the Commission would hold its own investigation.

The next order of business was the selection of a general counsel. The first person suggested for this position was rejected because he was "too controversial."[7] Warren then proposed J. Lee Rankin, a former Solicitor General of the United States, and the Commission "immediately and unanimously" agreed upon him.[8]

Finally the Commission decided to ask Waggoner Carr to postpone the Texas court of inquiry until the Commission had completed its investigation.[9] After the meeting Chief Justice Warren wrote to Carr on behalf of the Commission, stating:

> We are most anxious, as I am sure you are, to take no steps which could impede investigation or which could lead the public to mistaken conclusions based upon partial factual information.[10]

Warren further suggested that public hearings might prejudice the trial of Jack Ruby, and said that for these reasons the Commission felt that "a public inquiry in Texas at this time might be more harmful than helpful. . . ."[11] Warren then invited Carr and his special counsel to "participate in the Commission's work, and counsel with it."[12] Carr accepted the offer, and he (or his special counsel) attended most of the Commission hearings.

The General Counsel. On December 8 Warren called J. Lee Rankin in New York City and asked him to be general counsel for the Commission. It was understood that Rankin would organize the investigation for the Commission and be its "executive director" as well as its counsel.[13] Rankin left for Washington the next day and devoted the next ten months to Commission work.

Neither Rankin nor the Commission realized at the time how demanding the job would be.[14] Rankin not only superintended the investigation and the writing of the Report, but also examined most of the important witnesses who appeared before the Commission; he adjudicated the disputes that constantly arose among the staff lawyers; and he acted as liaison between the Commission and other government agencies.[15] Rankin found that he was "the man in the middle"; all the investigators' problems were passed through him up to the Commission; all the Commission's directives were passed through him down to the staff.[16] A member of the staff described it as "an extraordinary arrangement. Rankin was the only person the Commission would talk to; everything had to be funneled through him."[17]

Although they generally agreed that Rankin was a competent administrator, his soft-spoken and permissive manner led some of the staff lawyers to feel that he might "tone down" their arguments when presenting them before the Commission.[18] It was also felt that Rankin at times was "too responsive" to Warren and that he refused to "stand up" to the Commission.[19] These criticisms, however, failed to take into account the very basic fact that Rankin worked for the Commission.

On December 9 the FBI submitted a Summary Report of its investigation to the Commissioners. This four-volume report, which summarized the entire FBI investigation to date, was considered "of principal importance" in the formulation of the investigation.[20]

On December 13 Congress, in a Joint Resolution, empowered the Commission to subpoena witnesses and to compel their testimony by granting them immunity if they pleaded the Fifth Amendment. This latter power, however, was never used by the Commission.

The Second Meeting. The Commission met again on December 16. J. Lee Rankin was sworn in as General Counsel; henceforth he would sit in on all Commission meetings. The main purpose of this meeting was to determine the scope of the investigation.[21] First the FBI Summary Report was considered. This report paralleled, McCloy said "perhaps too closely," the Commission's mission of ascertaining the facts of the assassination, and thus the Commission decided to reserve judgment on the conclusion of the FBI Summary Report until all its premises were critically reappraised.[22] There was also some question as to whether the FBI report should be made public.[23] The Commission decided as policy that no evidence should be released before publication of the Commission's Report, because "piecemeal releases" might only serve to confuse the public and add to the irresponsible rumors.[24]

Although the investigation was to be "independent," the Commission decided to rely on federal agencies to conduct its basic investigation. Rankin explained that it would have been impractical for the Commission to attempt to recruit its own investigative force.[25] Dulles added that independent investigators would cause needless friction in dealing with government agencies and would complicate the security problem.[26] Furthermore, since the Commission had been promised the full cooperation of federal investigative agencies, it was deemed unnecessary "to employ investigators other than the legal staff."[27]

Finally the Commission decided to review thoroughly the investigative material on which the FBI had based its Summary Report.[28] Because this imposing task required assistance, Rankin was authorized to organize a staff of independent lawyers to help in analyzing these thousands of investigative reports and sorting out the issues that required verification or further investigation.[29] The Commission then planned to hold hearings to examine the more important witnesses and evidence.[30]

The Staff. The FBI investigative reports began arriving at the Commission's offices on December 20.[31] With the reports came Howard P. Willens, a young and energetic Department of Justice lawyer who was to play an important role in shaping the investigation. The then Deputy Attorney General, Nicholas deB. Katzenbach, had asked Willens to act as a liaison between the Commission and the Department of Justice. Willens said that his was supposed to have been a part-time job, but, upon seeing the amount of work that confronted the Commission, he returned to his office, "packed up" his desk, and moved into the Commission's offices.[32] Willens took charge of the administrative function; he divided up the work among the staff, made schedules, requested assistance from other agencies, and "kept the investigation moving."[33] Some considered him "hard-driving" and "aggressive"; others considered him "the hero of the investigation."[34]

Rankin chose Norman Redlich, a New York University law professor and an editor of *The Tax Law Review,* as his special assistant. Rankin said that Redlich had deep understanding of the law and was more than simply a lawyer or editor.[35] In addition, Redlich had the asset of tremendous energy; when necessary, he could work from 8 a.m. to 3 a.m., seven days a week.[36] Redlich, however, tended to be a "perfectionist," and this quality engendered some friction among the lawyers.

Some felt that Redlich was "unyielding on points of law," but most agreed that he made an important contribution to the Commission.

Both Redlich and Willens considered themselves to be Rankin's deputies, and, at first this caused some confusion. However, as the investigation progressed, Redlich became occupied with special projects—for example, preparing the examination of Marina Oswald—and Willens became occupied with day-to-day administrative problems.[37] Rankin, Willens, and Redlich, each in his own way, were indispensable to the work of the Commission, and each influenced the outcome of the investigation.

In late December, Rankin selected the "senior counsel" for the staff. He said that above all the commission wanted a "balanced" staff drawn from all parts of the country—lawyers whose reputations would add weight to the Report.[38] Rankin thus chose lawyers who were held in high esteem by their regional Bar Associations:

From New York City, Francis W. H. Adams, a former police commissioner and a leader in the Democratic Reform movement; from California, Joseph A. Ball, a well-known trial lawyer and a member of the United States Judiciary Conference Advisory Committee; from Philadelphia, William T. Coleman, Jr., a former special counsel for the City of Philadelphia, a consultant with the United States Arms Control and Disarmament Agency, and one of the best-known Negro lawyers in America; from New Orleans, Leon D. Hubert, Jr., a former United States attorney and professor at Tulane University; from Chicago, Albert E. Jenner, Jr., a former assistant attorney general for Illinois and vice-chairman of the National Joint Committee for the Effective Administration of Justice.

The criterion of professional eminence led not only to the selection of lawyers with outstanding reputations, but also to the selection of extremely busy lawyers. When Norman Redlich was asked how such men could have given up nine months of their practice, he answered, "Very simple. They didn't."[39] The lawyers were employed on a consulting basis, receiving $100 a day and expenses. Some of the senior counsel worked for the Commission for only a few days and lent their reputations but not their time.[40]

The bulk of the work devolved on the "junior counsel"— lawyers in their early thirties who had had distinguished law-school records and private practices.[41] Willens, who selected most of the junior counsel, said, "We wanted independent lawyers, not government men, who had been at the top of their class and who could work 16 hours a day."[42]

Melvin A. Eisenberg, a twenty-nine-year-old New York corporation lawyer who had been first in his class at Harvard, was chosen by Redlich as his assistant. Arlen Specter, a former assistant district attorney of Philadelphia and former co-editor of the *Yale Law Journal* (with Howard Willens), was the next lawyer selected. Samuel A. Stern, a Washington lawyer and a former law clerk to Chief Justice Earl Warren, and Burt W. Griffin, a former assistant United States attorney for the Northern District of Ohio, were also selected by Willens. David W. Belin, an Iowa trial lawyer, and W. David Slawson, a Denver lawyer, were both recommended to the Commission. Finally, Wesley J. Liebeler, a former Wall Street lawyer who considered himself "definitely not establishment" and who sometimes played the role of devil's advocate on the staff, was recommended to Willens by the dean of the University of Chicago Law School.[43]

The "junior counsel" also worked as consultants, receiving $75 a day and expenses. Rankin noted that, "unlike the senior lawyers who were losing money every day they worked, many of the junior lawyers were making more than they made in private practice."[44] In any event, the junior lawyers spent considerably more time on the case than did the senior lawyers.[45]

The Commission approved the lawyers on the basis of

short one-paragraph biographical statements that were submitted by Rankin. Commissioner Ford said, "We gave Rankin a free hand in selecting the staff. I trusted his judgment."[46]

The Organization. The three weeks from December 21 to January 10 were critical in the formulation of the investigation.[47] On December 28 Howard Willens drew up a memorandum which set forth the *modus operandi*.[48] This memorandum proposed that the investigation be divided into five separate areas. A senior and junior lawyer would be assigned to each area and would resolve the minor problems and inconsistencies in that area. Under this arrangement, only the major problems would be passed on to the Commission. After ascertaining the facts in its area, each team would prepare a draft chapter on its findings, and this would correspond to a chapter in the Report. The areas were arranged on a descending scale of generality. The first area was to be concerned with the basic facts of the assassination itself; the second area would narrow down its focus to the identity of the assassin. The third area would deal with Oswald's background and motives, while the fourth area would be concerned with possible conspiratorial relationships Oswald had. The fifth area would deal with the death of Oswald. A sixth area, Presidential protection, was later added at the request of the Commission.[49]

This plan, it should be noted, did not provide for a separate investigation into the murder of Dallas Policeman J. D. Tippit. Instead, the Tippit investigation was considered to be part of the Area II investigation of the identity of the President's assassin.[50]

Finally, the memorandum suggested that Marina Oswald, the alleged assassin's widow, be called as the first witness in the Commission hearing. This would give the lawyers additional time to recommend witnesses in their areas for the Commission hearings.[51]

Toward the end of December, Willens and Rankin arranged for the appointment of liaisons between the Commission and other government agencies cooperating in the investigation. Appointed were Inspector James J. Malley from the FBI, Inspector Thomas Kelley from the Secret Service, R. G. Rocca from the CIA, and Abram Chayes from the Department of State.[52]

January

The Sorting Process. As the lawyers arrrived in Washington during the first three weeks of January, they were assigned to areas by Willens and Rankin. Francis W. H. Adams and Arlen Specter, both of whom had considerable investigative experience, were assigned to Area I, "the basic facts of the assassination." Their principal job was to establish the source of the shots.[53]

Joseph Ball and David Belin, both experienced criminal trial lawyers, were assigned to Area II, "the identity of the assassin." Their task was to develop evidence which identified the assassin.[54] Albert Jenner and Wesley Liebeler were assigned to Area III, Oswald's background. Their job was to explore Oswald's life and to delineate factors which might have caused him to assassinate the President.[55]

William Coleman, who had considerable experience in dealing with government agencies, and W. David Slawson were assigned to Area IV, "possible conspiratorial relationships." Their main concern was Oswald's movements outside the country, and their task was to ascertain whether any other person or group influenced Oswald in the assassination.[56]

Two former United States attorneys, Leon Hubert and Burt Griffin, were assigned to Area V, "Oswald's death." They had two problems: to ascertain, first, whether Ruby had had any assistance in murdering Oswald, and, second, whether Ruby had had any prior connection with Oswald.[57]

Samuel Stern was assigned to Area VI, "Presidential protection." His task was to scrutinize the precautions taken by the Secret Service and FBI. J. Lee Rankin was nominally the senior counsel in this politically sensitive area.[58]

Each team of lawyers was assigned a secretary and an office in the Commission's headquarters at 200 Maryland Avenue N.E., conveniently located between the Supreme Court and Capitol Hill. Willens brought in two lawyers from the Department of Justice—Charles N. Shaffer, Jr., and Stuart R. Pollak—to assist with the clerical and administrative duties. (Francis Adams, apprehensive over the division of labor, privately warned Warren of a "burgeoning bureaucracy.") In the basement of the building the FBI installed a scale model of the assassination site, as well as film projectors and other necessary equipment.[59]

After the lawyers were organized into teams, the initial phase of the investigation, the sorting-out process, began. Willens divided the more than twenty thousand pages of investigative reports furnished by the FBI and Secret Service into areas and then parceled them out to the teams of lawyers concerned with each area. The teams then read, analyzed, and collated the relevant material in the reports, sorting out possible inconsistencies, unresolved questions, and matters that required further investigation.[60]

In the process of reducing the mass of investigative material to manageable proportions, there was the possibility that some pertinent information would be lost. Wesley Liebeler took the position that a lawyer in one area might not perceive the relevance of information to another area. Liebeler therefore suggested that one lawyer read all the reports.[61] Rankin replied that it was important to get the material into the hands of the lawyers charged with investigating it, and that later, "if time permitted," a member of the staff could read all the reports.[62]

The First Staff Meeting. At the first formal staff meeting, held in late January, Rankin told the lawyers. "Truth is your only client." He instructed them to gather the facts without forming conclusions and not to accept the FBI Summary Report as final.[63] The lawyers then were introduced to the Chief Justice, who cautioned them that their investigation might involve national security problems and asked them not to discuss their work outside the Commission.[64]

The Third Commission Meeting. The Commission met on January 21, mainly to discuss procedural questions. Hearings were to be held in February, and the immediate problem was to decide the form they would take. Would they be open or closed to the public?[65]

The Commission gave several reasons for its decision to hold closed hearings. One reason offered was that hearings open to the public "might interfere with Ruby's rights to a fair and impartial trial."[66] It is doubtful, however, if this was the decisive reason. Only a few witnesses (none of whose testimony pertained to Ruby) were called before the Ruby trial was completed.[67] If Ruby's trial had been the only consideration, the Commission could have held closed hearings until Ruby's trial was completed, and then held open hearings.

The Commission also expressed concern that open hearings "might prejudice innocent parties" if hearsay testimony were made public out of context.[68] It is not clear in this respect why the Commission hearings raised problems that Congressional hearings do not raise. The fact that the Commission *did* permit the most damaging type of hearsay evidence and allegations to be published eventually indicates that this was not a major reason.

The most substantial reason that the Commission gave was that, since testimony could not always be taken in logical sequence, it "was impractical and could be misleading" to hold public hearings.[69] This was also the main reason why Warren requested Waggoner Carr to postpone the Texas court of inquiry. Evidently the Commission was greatly concerned that the public might reach mistaken conclusions if testimony were released unevaluated and out of context.

Another problem faced at the third Commission meeting arose from a telegram sent by Mark Lane, a New York lawyer who claimed to represent the interests of Lee Harvey Oswald. Lane requested that he be appointed "defense counsel" for Oswald and be permitted to cross-examine the witnesses.[70] This request was rejected because the Commission considered itself to be an "impartial fact-finding agency," not a court, and thus there was no need for a "defense counsel."[71]

In addition, at this meeting the Commission approved a resolution "governing questioning of the witnesses by the members of the Commission staff."[72] And it was decided that Marina Oswald would be the Commission's first witness.[73]

The Problems. On the next day, January 22, Rankin was informed by Waggoner Carr, the Attorney General of Texas, of an allegation that Lee Harvey Oswald had been a paid FBI informer. Henry Wade, the Dallas District Attorney, had also heard this allegation.[74] Rankin immediately told Warren of this development, and an emergency meeting of the Commission was called for that afternoon.[75] The members began arriving at about 5:30 p.m. for what Representative Ford described as "the most tense and hushed meeting" he remembered.[76] The Commission decided to ask both Carr and Wade to come to Washington immediately.[77]

On January 24 Carr and Wade flew to Washington and met with Warren and Rankin. Neither of the Texas officials knew the source of the story, or if it was true, but they gave such details as Oswald's alleged informant number, his salary, and the time he was supposedly employed by the FBI.[78]

The Commission met again on January 27 to discuss the problem further. The decision was to inform the FBI of the allegation and at the same time to conduct an exhaustive investigation of Oswald's relations with government agencies.[79]

While the Commission was considering the problem of Oswald's alleged association with the FBI, the staff was faced with an equally serious problem stemming from the movie film of the assassination. This film was taken by Abraham Zapruder, an amateur photographer, and graphically shows virtually the entire assassination. In ten seconds of color film, the President is shown waving and smiling, then suddenly reaching for his throat and slowly slumping over. About a second later Governor Connally is apparently hit. About three seconds after that the fatal shot visibly strikes the President's head.[80] The film was first viewed by staff members on January 27, 1964; FBI experts and Secret Service agents attended the session.[81]

It became apparent, from a frame-by-frame analysis of the film, that the shots were not evenly spaced apart in time, as had been assumed. In fact, the first two shots seemed to hit Kennedy and Connally within a period of one and a half seconds. The proximity of these two shots raised doubts as to whether an assassin could possibly fire a bolt-action rifle two times in one and a half seconds.[82] This problem grew more complex as the investigation proceeded.

The Delay. At the end of January, Rankin told the staff that the field investigation would be postponed until the completion of the Ruby trial.[83] Rankin later explained that the Commission did not want to interfere with Ruby's rights, and that he felt more time was needed to prepare for the investigation.[84] Rankin instructed the staff to continue reading the in-

vestigative reports and to draw up preliminary plans for the
field investigation by March 1.[85]

February

The Hearings. The Commission hearings began on February 3 with the testimony of Marina Oswald. For the first four
days of the Commission's hearings J. Lee Rankin respectfully
and patiently questioned Mrs. Oswald about all aspects of
Oswald's life.[86] Her answers did not completely satisfy the
staff.

At the next staff meeting, on about February 6, some of
the lawyers requested that Marina Oswald be questioned
further. Rankin, however, announced that the Commission
had decided that they believed her and that there would be
no further questioning of her. The announcement precipitated
a heated argument in which one prominent lawyer threatened
to resign unless Mrs. Oswald was cross-examined. Rankin reportedly "lost control" of the meeting, and there were few formal staff meetings held after this one.[87]

Staff Meetings. Rankin said the staff meetings generated
"more heat than light."[88] And Howard Willens explained that
the reason only four or five staff meetings were held after
February was that they were not really necessary. He went on
to say that the Commission believed that this type of investigation could best be coordinated from the top and that there
was no reason, from an administrative point of view, for "all
the lawyers to discuss all aspects of every problem."[89]

Another staff dispute arose over the question of whether
or not witnesses should be "prepared." Trial lawyers usually
"prepare" a witness by discussing his story with him before
he testifies, in order to reduce inconsistencies and irrelevan-

cies. Norman Redlich pointed out that in the British system of commission inquiry witnesses testify without advance preparation, and he took the position that the Commission's witnesses should *not* be "prepared."[90] Most of the lawyers on the staff with trial experience thought that Redlich's position was impractical.[91] They maintained that if witnesses testified completely spontaneously the record would be confused with irrelevancies, and pertinent points might be obscured. Rankin appointed Redlich, Belin, and Liebeler to study this problem as a committee. A compromise was then worked out, in which lawyers were to submit memoranda containing their off-the-record conversations with witnesses.[92] When the investigation finally began, however, there was simply no time for preparing memoranda, and thus Rankin told the lawyers to use their own discretion in preparing witnesses.[93]

Goldberg and Craig. In late February, Alfred Goldberg, a senior United States Air Force historian, joined the staff. Warren apparently wanted the Report to have a historic as well as a legal perspective.[94] Goldberg, who worked directly under Rankin, was to play a major role in writing the report. He was also assigned the task of preparing a "Speculation and Rumor" appendix.[95]

On February 25 the Commission asked Walter E. Craig, President of the American Bar Association, to advise the Commission whether "the proceedings conformed to the basic principles of American justice."[96] Apparently the position taken at the January 21 meeting, that the Commission was a fact-finding agency and not a court, was reconsidered. The record indicates, however, that Craig's assignment was no more than a formality.

The Commission heard only four witnesses during February: Oswald's widow and her business manager, James H. Martin; Oswald's mother; and Oswald's brother. Waiting for the Ruby trial to end and the staff's field investigation to begin, the Commission heard no substantive evidence concerning the assassination itself.

March

The Investigation. During the first two weeks in March the lawyers continued preparing the material in their areas. Each team prepared a list of witnesses to be called during its field investigation, and these lists were submitted to Rankin for his *pro forma* approval.[97] The teams sent questions that required further investigation to Willens, who forwarded them to the FBI, the Secret Service, or the CIA. When questions arose as to the operations of government agencies, the teams prepared questionnaires for the agencies concerned.[98] The lawyers also outlined the major problems in their areas and drew up preliminary plans of attack. These plans did not necessarily have to be submitted to Rankin, who explained that he wanted lawyers "to be independent and have a free hand" in their own areas.[99] One lawyer commented that the preparations were so hectic that there wasn't time for formal agendas and the lawyers were thus forced "to play it by ear."[100]

On March 14 the Ruby trial ended and the investigation proper began. On March 18 Willens, Ball, and Belin flew to Dallas and laid the groundwork for the field investigation.[101] Willens arranged facilities for the staff in the United States Attorney's offices in the Post Office building. Barefoot Sanders, Jr., the United States Attorney for Dallas, acted as liaison between the Commission and the Texas authorities.[102]

Meanwhile, Ball and Belin informally interviewed police officials and the key witnesses to the assassination, and Ball arranged for some of the eyewitnesses to appear before the Commission in Washington the following week.[103]

On March 20 Ball and Belin conducted an off-the-record reconstruction of Oswald's assumed movements at the scene of the assassination. Most of the eyewitnesses who were to appear before the Commission participated in this re-enactment.[104]

By March 23 most of the lawyers had arrived in Dallas to conduct their field investigations. These investigations consisted mainly of taking depositions from witnesses whom the lawyers had selected after reading the investigative reports. In the depositions, each witness was sworn in and then examined by a lawyer.

The Hearings. While the staff was conducting its field investigation in Dallas, the "more important" eyewitnesses to the assassination testified at the Commission hearings. The Commission held a total of fourteen days of hearings in March; the most unusual hearing took place on March 4, when Mark Lane testified. Lane asked to be heard in an open hearing, and the Commission granted his request.[105] Ironically, this hearing took place on the day that the Ruby trial opened, and the Commission permitted Lane to give hearsay testimony concerning an alleged meeting that took place in Ruby's nightclub.[106]

Staff Changes. As the investigation progressed, it was necessary to alter the staff organization. Francis W. H. Adams, the senior lawyer in Area I, was unable to participate in the investigation, and the junior lawyer, Arlen Specter, had to manage this broad area singlehanded.[107] William Coleman also was unable to work full time for the Commission, and Stuart R. Pollak, a young Justice Department lawyer, was assigned to Coleman's area.[108] Because Ball and Belin were fully occupied with their investigation in Dallas, Eisenberg, who had been Redlich's assistant, was given the job of examining expert witnesses at Commission hearings.[109] John Hart

Ely, a Supreme Court law clerk, was appointed to the staff and assigned to help Jenner and Liebeler develop Oswald's biography.[110]

The Staff's Image of the Commission. By the end of March it became apparent to the lawyers that there were actually two separate investigations, the Commission hearings and the staff investigation.[111] Opinions differ as to what the Commission actually did. Joseph Ball commented that the Commission "had no idea of what was happening, we did all the investigating, lined up the witnesses, solved the problems and wrote the Report."[112] Wesley Liebeler, when asked what the Commission did, replied, "In one word, 'Nothing.' "[113] Melvin Eisenberg compared the Commission to a corporation's board of directors, with Rankin as president and the staff members as the officers.[114] Howard Willens reflected the consensus of the staff when he said, "The commissioners were not in touch with the investigation at all times."[115] J. Lee Rankin, on the other hand, said that some of the younger lawyers "simply didn't understand how a government inquiry worked" and that the Commission, through its experience and collective wisdom, gave the investigation its direction and focus.[116]

In any case, there was little direct contact between the Commissioners and the staff lawyers, and to most of the lawyers "Warren was the Commission."[117]

April

The investigation continued in Dallas during the first two weeks of April. Almost one-half of all the depositions taken by the staff were taken in this period. During this time Ball, assisted by Goldberg, Belin, Stern, and Ely, tried to establish Oswald's movements from the time of the assassination until his arrest;[118] Hubert and Griffin investigated Oswald's death; and Liebeler and Jenner, by interviewing Oswald's acquaintances and relatives, tried to cast light on Oswald's motive.[119]

In Washington, Specter and Redlich were concerned with the problem emanating from the film of the assassination. Rifle tests had established that the murder weapon could not fire two bullets within the time period during which the film showed that both Kennedy and Connally were hit. Specter then advanced the hypothesis that both men were hit by the same bullet. To test this hypothesis, he arranged wound ballistics experiments and further analyses of the film.[120]

Hearings. The Commission held only seven days of hearings in April. Probably the most important witness to testify was Governor Connally. Connally testified, as will be more fully discussed later, that it was "inconceivable" that he was hit by the bullet that hit Kennedy. His testimony, and other evidence, cast considerable doubt on the single-bullet hypothesis.

May

The Deadline. At a staff meeting in early May, Rankin told the lawyers to "wrap up" their investigations and to submit their chapters by June 1.[121] The deadline for releasing the Report was June 30.[122]

Some teams, however, had not yet resolved important problems in their areas, and others had turned up new evidence that required further investigation. In addition, the FBI had not yet answered a number of questions that the staff had submitted.[123] In short, the investigation was nowhere near completion.

On May 24 Rankin, Redlich, and Specter went to Dallas

to supervise an elaborate re-enactment of the assassination. A limousine with stand-ins for the President and Governor Connally took part in the simulation of the event. The main purpose of this reconstruction was to test the theory that both men were hit by a single bullet.[124]

The Commission held only four days of hearings in May. These meetings were mainly concerned with governmental processes.

Publishing. In late May, Warren announced that the supporting volumes of testimony and evidence would not be published.[125] The reason given was that it would be too expensive in view of the Commission's limited financing.[126] A number of lawyers believed, however, that the Commission was obliged to publish this material, and they protested the decision to Rankin. Rankin then called Senator Russell, who apparently did not know of Warren's decision.[127] The Congressional members of the Commission reportedly considered the expense justified, and the Commission agreed to publish what was to become twenty-six volumes of hearings and exhibits.[128]

June

Despite the June 1 deadline, only two lawyers had completed their draft chapters by the middle of June. Specter had submitted his chapter on the source of the shots by June 1, and Ball had turned in his chapter on the identification of the assassin the following week. Redlich, who had editorial responsibility for the chapters concerning the assassination, found Ball's chapter to be "inadequate," and over Ball's protests he undertook to rewrite it himself.[129]

The Commission reportedly was not apprised of the situation, and, as the date approached for releasing the Report,

Willens and Redlich went over Rankin's head and told Warren that some of the lawyers still had not completed their investigations and that it was impossible for the Report to be completed by June 30. Warren then reportedly lost his temper and demanded that Willens close down the investigation immediately.[130] The deadline was, however, extended to July 15.[131]

Hearings. On June 5 Mrs. John F. Kennedy testified before the Chief Justice at her home. She was the last witness to testify on the assassination itself.

On June 7 the Chief Justice and Commissioner Ford went to Dallas to hear the testimony of Jack Ruby. Afterward Warren and Ford spent about two hours at the scene of the assassination.[132]

On June 17 the Commission announced that it had completed its hearings.[133] Ten days later it was announced that the Report would not be released until after the Republican National Convention, which was to begin on July 13.[134]

July

As the summer dragged on, most of the lawyers left Washington and continued working for the Commission only on a very limited part-time basis. All five senior lawyers—Adams, Coleman, Ball, Hubert, and Jenner, in that order—had returned to their private practices and made virtually no contribution to the writing of the final Report.[135] Of the junior lawyers, only Liebeler, Griffin, and Slawson continued working for the Commission on a full-time basis.[136]

The major responsibility for writing the Report devolved on two men, Norman Redlich and Alfred Goldberg. Redlich, who worked up to eighteen hours a day, seven days a week, said on reflection, "It was very depressing; it seemed as if it would go on forever."[137] Goldberg told Warren that it was "impossible" to finish the Report by the July 15 deadline, and the deadline was extended to August 1.[138]

The Colloquium. Because there was strong disagreement among the staff on the use of psychological terminology to describe Oswald's actions, Rankin arranged for three psychiatrists to meet with staff and Commission members to discuss the problem. After a colloquium that lasted an entire day, the lawyers concluded that there was insufficient basis for drawing psychological conclusions about Oswald.[139]

On July 20 Liebeler submitted his chapter on Oswald's motives. Redlich and Rankin thought that it was "too psychological," and Goldberg was given the task of rewriting it.[140]

August

Throughout the month of August, Goldberg and Redlich continued writing and rewriting chapters. These were submitted first to Rankin and then to the individual Commissioners, after which they were sent back to the staff for additional rewriting. Some chapters were rewritten as many as twenty times by nearly as many hands. The problem of getting consensus seemed almost impossible, and bit by bit the August deadline was extended into September.[141]

Meanwhile, the pressures to publish the Report increased. Rankin reportedly received frequent calls from McGeorge Bundy of the White House staff,[142] and most of the Commissioners considered it was absolutely necessary for the Report to be released well before the Presidential election, lest the assassination become a political issue.[143]

September

On September 4 the galley proofs of the final draft were circulated among the Commission and staff for final comments. Two days later Wesley Liebeler submitted a twenty-six-page memorandum attacking the key chapter involving the identity of the assassin. The chapter had to be revised.[144]

The Final Hearing. On September 7 Commissioners Russell, Cooper, and Boggs went to Dallas to re-examine Marina Oswald. Under Senator Russell's rigorous questioning, she changed major aspects of her story and altered her previous testimony. More rewriting was thus necessitated.[145]

Finally, on September 24, the Report was submitted to President Johnson.[146]

At a farewell dinner the next day, the Chief Justice told the staff that its relationship to the government was analogous to "a lawyer-client relationship," thus suggesting that the lawyers' knowledge of the Commission and investigation was privileged information.[147]

On September 28, 1964, ten months after the Commission was created, the Warren Report was made public. Having completed its task, the Commission dissolved itself.[148]

PART ONE

Political Truth

2

The Dominant Purpose

THE PURPOSE OF the Commission was never fully stated in its Report. The executive order which created the Commission listed the "purposes" as examining evidence, conducting further investigations, evaluating the facts and circumstances, and reporting the findings to the President.[1] This order told what things the Commission was to do, but not *why* it was to do them. There is, however, an important distinction to be made between the function of the Commission, which was to ascertain the facts, and its ultimate purpose, which influenced the Commission's approach to its work, either consciously or unconsciously.

Chief Justice Warren gave only the formal purpose of the Commission when he stated, "The purpose of this Commission is, of course, eventually to make known to the President, and to the American public everything that has transpired before this Commission."[2] However, ascertaining the facts is not usually in itself a legitimate purpose for a government investigation. Warren himself had stated in the Supreme Court decision of *Watkins* v. *United States*: "No inquiry is an end in itself," and concluded that a Congressional investigation cannot "expose for the sake of exposure."[3] The Warren Commission was no doubt an extraordinary commission created in an extraordinary situation. The paramount purpose may well have been simply to make the truth known, but the question remains: Why?

The circumstances surrounding the Chief Justice's appointment to the Commission suggest the underlying purpose. Anthony Lewis, then *The New York Times* Supreme Court correspondent, reported that when Warren was first asked to serve on the Commission "he flatly said no." President Johnson then called Warren to the White House and spoke to him "about patriotism, about the new President's urgent need to settle the assassination rumors, about the special trust people in foreign lands would have in an investigation over which he presided." Warren thereupon agreed to serve on the Commission.[4] J. Lee Rankin confirmed this account and said that "Warren accepted, only with the greatest reluctance, because the President had made it plain to him that the nation's prestige was at stake."[5] These accounts clearly imply that one purpose of the Commission was to protect the national interest by settling "assassination rumors" and restoring American prestige abroad.

Other members of the Commission also conceived of the Commission's purpose in terms of the national interest. Allen Dulles said that an atmosphere of rumors and suspicion interferes with the functioning of the government, especially abroad, and one of the main tasks of the Commission was to dispel rumors.[6] John J. McCloy said that it was of paramount importance to "show the world that America is not a banana republic, where a government can be changed by conspiracy."[7] Senator John Sherman Cooper said that one of the Commission's most important purposes was "to lift the cloud of doubts that had been cast over American institutions."[8] Congressman Gerald Ford said that dispelling damaging rumors was a major concern of the Commission,[9] and most members of the Commission agreed.

There was thus a dualism in purpose. If the explicit purpose of the Commission was to ascertain and expose the facts, the implicit purpose was to protect the national interest by dispelling rumors.

These two purposes were compatible so long as the damaging rumors were untrue. But what if a rumor damaging to the national interest proved to be true? The Commission's explicit purpose would dictate that the information be exposed regardless of the consequences, while the Commission's implicit purpose would dictate that the rumor be dispelled regardless of the fact that it was true. In a conflict of this sort, one of the Commission's purposes would emerge as dominant.

The Dilemma

The Commission was, in fact, faced with just such a conflict at its meeting on January 27. The subject of this meeting was the allegation that Oswald had been a paid informer of the FBI.[10]

Three days earlier Chief Justice Warren and J. Lee Rankin had met secretly with Texas Attorney General Waggoner Carr and Dallas District Attorney Henry Wade.[11] The Texas officials related a story alleging that Oswald had been working for the FBI as an informant since September 1962;

that Oswald was on the FBI payroll at $200 a month on the day he was arrested; and that Oswald had been assigned an informant number, 179.[12] The source of the story seemed to be Alonzo Hudkins, a Houston newspaper reporter.[13]

Neither Carr nor Wade knew whether the story had any basis in fact, but Wade, a former FBI agent, had some reason to believe that there might have been a connection between Oswald and the FBI. Wade had apparently heard that Oswald's address book contained the telephone number and license-plate number of Dallas FBI agent James Hosty.[14] The Commission had received the list of names in Oswald's address book in a December 21, 1963, FBI report, but Agent Hosty's name had been omitted from that list by the FBI.[15] Wade also had heard that a government voucher for $200 was found in Oswald's possession.[16] In addition, a Western Union employee had claimed that Oswald was periodically telegraphed small sums of money. Also, Wade thought that Oswald's practice of setting up postal-box "covers" each time he moved—a practice Wade himself had used as an FBI agent—was an "ideal way" to handle undercover transactions.[17]

The Commission heard the full allegation at its January 27 meeting. Commissioner Ford observed: "The Commission itself had not grounds at the moment for rejecting or accepting [the rumor]. Members simply knew that the whole business was a most delicate and sensitive matter involving the nation's faith in its own institutions and one of the most respected federal agencies."[18]

J. Lee Rankin presented the problem to the Commission in no uncertain terms, stating:

> We do have a dirty rumor that is very bad for the Commission, the problem, and it is very damaging to the agencies that are involved in it and it must be wiped out insofar as it is possible to do so by this Commission.[19]

Quite clearly, the problem was the "dirty rumor." It was considered "dirty" not because it was known to be untrue but because it was known to be "damaging" to the government. The solution proposed was to "wipe out" the rumor. This would satisfy the implicit purpose of the Commission.

In this particular case, if the rumor was true, making the truth known might very well result in irreparable damage to the FBI and might heighten suspicions and speculations about the assassination itself. On the other hand, dispelling the rumor, even if it was true, would protect the national interest. Ford stated aptly that "the dilemma of the Commission" was how to approach this problem.[20]

Allen Dulles observed that the allegation was "a terribly hard thing to disprove," because written records were not always kept on undercover agents.[21] "If this be true," Hale Boggs responded, "[it] make[s] our problem utterly impossible, because you say this rumor can't be dissipated under any circumstances."[22] Again, the problem was seen as one of dispelling rumors.

Two Approaches

The Commission's approach to the problem had to be consistent with the national interest. Ford wrote that the Commission "would not be justified in plunging into the matter in some irresponsible manner that might jeopardize the effectiveness of an important agency's future operations."[23] This precept suggests a limiting case for the Commission's explicit purpose of making the truth known; would the Commission be justified in exposing information that would most certainly damage the future operations of an agency as important as the FBI?

J. Lee Rankin proposed that the Commission permit the FBI to investigate the matter and "clear its own skirts" *before* the Commission investigated it. He suggested that he personally should speak to J. Edgar Hoover and

> tell him this problem and that he should have as much interest as the Commission in trying to put an end to any such speculations, not only by his statement . . . but also if it were possible to demonstrate by whatever records and materials they have that it just couldn't be true.[24]

Rankin said that he would also tell Hoover that the Commission would reserve the right to investigate the matter further "if it found it necessary, in order to satisfy the American people that this question of an undercover agent was out of the picture."[25]

Although apparently there was considerable support for this course of action, two Commissioners were not entirely satisfied by it. Senator John Sherman Cooper suggested an alternate approach in which the Commission would apprise Hoover of the facts but at the same time pursue its own independent investigation into the rumor. Cooper said that the Commission was "under a duty to see what Hudkins [the immediate source of the rumor] says about it, where he got that information."[26] Senator Richard Russell agreed, saying:

> Of course, we can get an affidavit from Mr. Hoover and put it in this record and go on and act on that, but if we didn't go any further than that, and we don't pursue it down to Hudkins or whoever it is, there still would be thousands of doubting Thomases who would believe this man was an FBI agent. . . .[27]

Thus two approaches were proposed. Rankin had suggested that Hoover be given the opportunity to disprove the rumor *before* the Commission investigated it; Senators Cooper and Russell had suggested that the Commission fully investigate the rumor while informing Hoover of its course of action.

The Chief Justice then concluded: "We must go into this thing from both ends, from the end of the rumor-mongers and from the end of the FBI, and if we come into a *cul de sac*— well, there we are, but we can report on it."[28]

Warren's concern for "security" was possibly reflected in a statement he made to newspaper reporters less than a week after the meeting. On February 4 a reporter asked him if the full report was to be made public; Warren replied: "Yes, there will come a time. But it might not be in your lifetime. I am not referring to anything especially but there may be some things that would involve security."[29]

Although the Commissioners' discussion of this problem gives some insight into the Commission's dominant purpose, conclusions cannot be based on what are, in fact, selected and possibly out-of-context statements. Certainly the purpose of dispelling rumors was evident in the dialogue, but great concern was also shown by Senators Russell and Cooper for investigating the matter fully. The dominant purpose becomes clear not so much from the dialogue as from the Commission's subsequent course of action.

The day following the Commission meeting, Rankin discussed the allegation with J. Edgar Hoover. Hoover immediately assured Rankin that "any and every informant" was known to FBI headquarters and that "Oswald had never been an informant of the FBI."[30]

On February 6 Hoover submitted an affidavit to the Commission, stating that a search of FBI records disclosed that Oswald "was never an informant of the FBI, was never assigned a symbol number in that capacity, and was never paid

any amount of money in any regard."[31] A week later Hoover
sent the Commission the affidavits of ten FBI agents who had
had contact with the Oswald case; each denied that Oswald
was ever developed or used as an informant.[32] On February
27 Special Agent Robert Gemberling submitted an affidavit
explaining why the FBI, in its December 23 report,[33] had deleted the name of FBI agent James P. Hosty from the list of
names in Oswald's address book. According to Hoover, this
was done because "the circumstances under which Hosty's
name, et cetera, appeared in Oswald's notebook were fully
known to the FBI."[34]

On May 6 Alan H. Belmont, assistant director of the FBI,
appeared before the Commission and offered to leave Oswald's
file with the Commission. Rankin advised the Commission to
retain the file, although the staff would *not* be permitted to examine it. This was ordered so that "the Commission could say
in its report, 'We have seen everything that they [the FBI]
have.' "[35] Warren, however, refused to accept the file, saying:

> Well, the same people who would demand that we see
> everything of this kind would also demand they they be
> entitled to see it, and if it is a security matter we can't let
> them see it.[36]

The file thus was returned to the FBI, and, according to Samuel Stern, the lawyer in charge of the area, no independent
check was ever made of it.[37]

Finally, on May 14, J. Edgar Hoover testified before the
Commission and again categorically stated that Oswald had
no connection with the FBI.[38]

Although this latter approach produced very authoritative denials of the allegation, it amounted to no more than taking the FBI's word that Oswald did not work for them. Cer-

tainly, if the rumor was true, it was possible that the FBI would have admitted it. But, since such an admission might severely shake "the nation's faith in its own institutions" and jeopardize the future effectiveness of the FBI, it was in the national interest, as well as the FBI's interest, to deny this allegation in any case. As Rankin pointed out to the Commission, the FBI had an interest in ending the rumor.

Despite the fact that the Commission had agreed to approach the allegation from "both ends" and to hear Alonzo Hudkins, the source of the story, Hudkins was never called as a witness or questioned by the staff. Instead, Leon Jaworski, Special Counsel for the State of Texas, was asked to speak informally to Hudkins about the rumor.[39] According to Rankin, Jaworski reported back to the Commission that "there was absolutely nothing to the story" and that it was "sheer speculation based on nothing but Hudkins' imagination."[40] It was thus decided it was unnecessary to call Hudkins as a witness or to pursue the matter further from that end.[41]

There was, however, other evidence that suggested that Hudkins *did* have an actual source for his information. On January 24, three days prior to the Commission meeting, the Secret Service submitted about thirty investigative reports to the Commission.[42] One of these reports, carrying the control number 767, contained a Secret Service interview with Hudkins. Hudkins told the Secret Service agents that his information came from Allan Sweatt, the chief of the criminal division of the Dallas sheriff's office.[43] According to Hudkins, Sweatt stated:

Oswald was being paid two hundred dollars per month by the FBI in connection with their subversive investigation [and] that Oswald had informant number S-172.[44]

Allan Sweatt was never questioned by the Commission or its staff. The Commission apparently never attempted to ascertain Sweatt's source for the information or whether he had direct knowledge of the FBI's subversive investigation in Dallas.[45] In addition, no effort was made to clarify the nature of the FBI's subversive investigation or to determine whether there was any relationship between the Cuban exile groups which Oswald had been trying to infiltrate and the groups which interested the FBI.[46] Also, no check was made of the FBI files to see if number S-172 (or 179) possibly could have been assigned to Oswald.[47]

In short, no efforts were made by the Commission or its staff to investigate the rumor itself.

The Commission thus did exactly what it agreed *not* to do in its meeting; it relied entirely on the FBI to disprove the rumor.

The important question is not whether or not Oswald was employed by the FBI. Even if he had been an FBI informant—and no evidence developed to substantiate this possibility—this fact might not be particularly relevant to the assassination itself, although it might have explained Oswald's movements prior to the assassination. However, the important question is: How did the Commission choose to deal with a potentially damaging rumor?

Two courses of action were open to the Commission. It could have investigated the rumor itself and called as witnesses the persons known to be the immediate sources of the rumor. This approach quite probably would have exhausted the rumor, but it *might* have revealed information damaging to the national interest.

On the other hand, the Commission could have turned the whole matter over to the FBI.

This approach would not only have served to dispel the rumor, but would also have ensured that no damaging information would be revealed in the process unless the agency concerned itself chose to reveal it.

In the end, the Commission took the second approach. The entire matter was turned over to the FBI, to affirm or deny, and the Commission relied solely on the FBI's word in concluding that "there was absolutely no type of informant or undercover relationship" between Oswald and the FBI.

The way the Commission dealt with this problem cannot be explained simply in terms of its explicit purpose of making known to the President and the American public everything that went on before it. Nowhere, not even in the "Speculations and Rumors" appendix, does the Report mention the allegation that had so preoccupied the Commission. Nor does the information Carr and Wade furnished on January 24 appear anywhere in the Commission procedings.[48] Furthermore, the Secret Service interview with Hudkins has been withheld even from the National Archives.[49] And details of the problem were kept secret even from some staff lawyers for a time.[50] Quite clearly, the Commission handled the problem in such a way that it would *not* be made known.

The Commission's treatment of this problem was, however, consistent with the purpose of dispelling damaging rumors. If the Commission had called Hudkins and Sweatt as witnesses and fully investigated the allegation, the result very well might have heightened doubts and suspicions. If the Commission had disclosed the information furnished by Wade, Carr, and the Secret Service reports, the disclosure most probably would have led to new rumors and speculations. The surest and safest way to dispel the rumor was *not* to investigate it, but to keep secret the allegations and publish only the affidavits of denial. The Commission's course of action in this case can thus be explained only in terms of the purpose of dispelling damaging rumors. The fact that the Commission chose this approach, despite its earlier rejection of it, indicates the pervasiveness of this purpose.

Furthermore, the extent to which the purpose of dispelling rumors dominated the investigation is of critical importance to an understanding of the Commission's workings and decisions.

3

The Vulnerability of Facts

By EARLY February 1964 it became evident that it was possible for a lone gunman to have accomplished the assassination if and only if President Kennedy and Governor Connally were hit by the same bullet. "To say that they were hit by separate bullets," a Commission lawyer stated bluntly, "is synonymous with saying that there were two assassins."[1] This conclusion stemmed from an analysis of the movie film of the assassination.

A frame-by-frame analysis of the Zapruder film shows three distinct moments of reaction: frame no. 225 (President Kennedy raises his hands to his throat); frame no. 235 (Governor Connally slumps forward); and frame no. 313 (bullet strikes the President's head). By this analysis, only ten frames, or about one-half second (at the camera speed established by

43

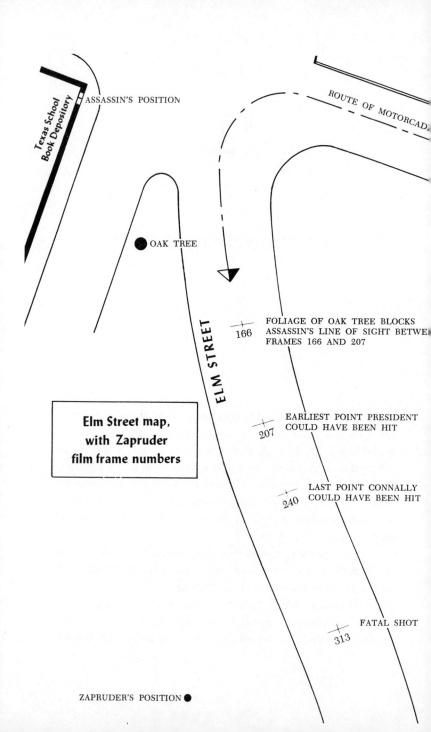

Texas School Book Depository

ASSASSIN'S POSITION

ROUTE OF MOTORCADE

OAK TREE

ELM STREET

Elm Street map, with Zapruder film frame numbers

166 — FOLIAGE OF OAK TREE BLOCKS ASSASSIN'S LINE OF SIGHT BETWEEN FRAMES 166 AND 207

207 — EARLIEST POINT PRESIDENT COULD HAVE BEEN HIT

240 — LAST POINT CONNALLY COULD HAVE BEEN HIT

313 — FATAL SHOT

ZAPRUDER'S POSITION ●

laboratory tests as 18.3 frames per second), elapsed between the time both men were first apparently wounded.

It is possible that both men had delayed reactions to the shots, but even in this case the maximum time between the first two shots could still be fixed. Since an oak tree's foliage obstructed the line of fire between film frames 166 and 207 (see map on facing page), and other evidence shows that the President could not have been shot before film frame 166, the Commission concluded that the earliest point that the President could have been first hit was film frame 207.[2] Medical experts, including Connally's doctors, established with certainty, and the Commission agreed, that Connally was not in a position to be hit after film frame 240.[3] Thus the maximum time that could have elapsed between the times both men were first shot was 33 film frames or about 1.8 seconds.

However, it was also established that the minimum time in which the assassination weapon could be fired twice was 2.3 seconds (or 42 film frames).[4] This minimum figure was based on the length of time required to open and close the bolt of the rifle (and did not include the aiming time).[5]

Thus, according to the established facts, it was physically impossible for the assassination rifle to have been fired twice during the time period when the President and Governor Connally were first wounded. Either both men were hit by the same bullet, or there were two assassins.

The Autopsy Report

The answer to the crucial question of whether it was *possible* for both men to have been hit by the same bullet depended on the findings of the autopsy, conducted on the night of the assassination at the Bethesda Naval Hospital in Maryland. Quite simply, if the autopsy had found that the bullet which struck the President in the back had exited from the front of his body, then it was possible that the bullet continued on to hit Connally, who was seated in front of Kennedy. If, however, the autopsy revealed that the bullet had *not* exited from the front of the President's body, it was obviously impossible for both men to have been hit by the same bullet.

Although "certain preliminary draft notes" relating to the autopsy were subsequently destroyed,[6] the Commission published what purported to be the original "Autopsy Report" as an appendix to the Warren Report.[7] This autopsy report says:

> The missile contused the strap muscle of the right side of the neck, damaged the trachea [windpipe] and made its exit through the anterior surface of the neck.[8]

The Commission's autopsy report clearly states that the bullet exited from the front of the President's neck, and thus it was possible for the same bullet to have hit Governor Connally. (The Warren Report explained that a previous theory that the bullet lodged in the President's strap muscles and later fell out onto his stretcher was disproved and rejected "during the autopsy").[9]

The Commission's autopsy report, however, differs substantially from earlier reports of the autopsy findings. On December 18, 1963, more than three weeks after the autopsy, the *Washington Post* reported that the autopsy had found that the bullet did *not* exit from the President's neck, and that the throat wound was caused by a fragment from a third shot which had hit the President's head.[10] Similar versions of the autopsy findings appeared in most of the major newspapers and medical journals.[11] *The New York Times*, citing a source familiar with the autopsy report, stated:

The first bullet made what was described as a small, neat wound in the back and penetrated two or three inches. . . . The pathologists at Bethesda, the source said, concluded that the throat wound was caused by the emergence of a metal fragment or piece of bone resulting from the fatal shot in the head.[12]

If this version was in error, it was not immediately corrected. As late as January 26, 1964, *The New York Times* reported that investigators were satisfied that the first bullet hit the President in the back and that "that bullet lodged in his shoulder."[13]

Newspaper accounts are often inaccurate; the fact that this story was widely circulated does not necessarily mean that the original source was accurate. These newspaper accounts therefore cannot be accepted as evidence, but they do raise a question as to whether the autopsy report published in the Warren Report was in fact the *original* one.

The FBI Summary Report and the FBI Supplemental Report

There is one document, however, which casts considerably more light on this question: the FBI Summary Report. Immediately after the assassination, President Johnson ordered the FBI to conduct a complete investigation and report its findings to him.[14] In early December, J. Edgar Hoover submitted to President Johnson through the Attorney General a four-volume report summarizing the FBI's investigation.[15] On December 9 these volumes were submitted to the Commission; a fifth volume, subtitled "Supplemental Report," was sent to the Commission on January 13, 1964. Considered "of principal importance" by the Commission, the FBI Summary Report (with the supplement) was an authoritative and official summary of the facts as of January 13, 1964, before the Commission began its work.*[16]

With regard to the autopsy, the December 9 FBI Summary Report states:

> Medical examination of the President's body revealed that one of the bullets had entered just below his shoulder to the right of the spinal column at an angle of 45 to 60 degrees downward, that there was no point of exit, and that the bullet was not in the body.[17]

The FBI Summary Report thus says unequivocally that the bullet in question had not exited from the front of the President's body; it implies that the bullet had fallen out onto the President's stretcher while he was in the hospital in Dallas.[18]

The Warren Report thus directly contradicts the FBI Summary Report on the autopsy findings. The possibility of a clerical error or misinterpretation in the December 9 FBI Summary Report is diminished by the FBI Supplemental Report, dated January 13, which states:

> Medical examination of the President's body had revealed that the bullet which entered his back had penetrated to a distance of less than a finger length.[19]

"Medical examination of the President's body" can have referred only to the Bethesda autopsy of November 22; *before* the autopsy, the bullet hole was not discovered; and after the autopsy, there was no further medical examination.[20] The FBI Summary Report and the Supplemental Report thus say, in

---

*These volumes have not hitherto been made public. Because of their pertinence to the subject of this book, substantial portions of them are reproduced here as Appendices A and B (see pp. 155 *ff.*).

short, that the autopsy revealed that the bullet did *not* exit from the President's neck, and that it penetrated the President's back to the depth of only a few inches. How can such a contradiction on such an essential point be explained?

There can be no doubt that the autopsy findings were known to the FBI when it prepared the Summary Report. Two FBI agents were present at the autopsy.[21] The autopsy report was forwarded to the FBI.[22] Moreover, at the time the autopsy was performed, the FBI was the only agency charged with ascertaining all the facts of the assassination.

Arlen Specter, the Commission staff lawyer who developed the autopsy evidence, explained that the doctors were unable at first to find the bullet's path through the President's body. At this point, he said, both FBI agents "rushed out of the room" and telephoned the result to their Maryland field office. Meanwhile, according to Specter, the doctors found the path, but by the time the agents submitted their reports the FBI Summary Report had "gone to press."[23]

There are, however, a number of problems inherent in this explanation. First of all, there exists Secret Service testimony that one FBI agent remained in the room at all times.[24] Second, two Secret Service agents, who were also in the room throughout the autopsy, indicated in their testimony that no path was found through the body.[25] Third, the December 9 FBI Summary Report could not possibly have gone to press until at least eleven days after the autopsy of November 22.[26] Finally, Specter's story in no way explains why the FBI Supplemental Report (dated January 13) also states that the autopsy revealed that the bullet penetrated to a depth of less than a finger length.

The Dilemma

Clearly, the FBI Summary and Supplemental Reports and the Warren Report give diametrically opposed findings regarding the President's autopsy. This presents a dilemma. On one hand, if the FBI reports distorted such a basic fact of the assassination, doubt is cast on the accuracy of the FBI's *entire* investigation; indeed the Commission's investigation and conclusions were, in the final analysis, predicated on the accuracy of the FBI reports.

The second horn of the dilemma is even more painful, for, if the FBI's statements on the autopsy are accurate, then the autopsy findings must have been changed after January 13. This would mean that the document in the Warren Report which purports to be the original autopsy report is not.

This dilemma cannot be resolved in terms of what one considers to be "inconceivable." To some it would be "inconceivable" that the FBI would make a repeated error of this magnitude and import in its final report to the President; to others it would be inconceivable that the Warren Commission would substantially alter the basic facts. The answer may, however, be found in the evidence surrounding the autopsy.

The Evidence

Consistency with the evidence does not necessarily prove validity, but inconsistency *does* prove invalidity. The FBI Summary and Supplemental Reports and the Warren Report give diametrically opposed versions of the autopsy; both versions can be measured against the evidence to determine which is invalid.

The FBI Summary and Supplemental Reports claim that the autopsy revealed that: (1) the first bullet entered "just below [the President's] shoulder," (2) it penetrated "less than a finger length," and (3) "there was no point of exit." The Warren Report claims that the autopsy revealed that the first bullet: (1) entered the "rear of the neck," (2) passed completely through the neck, and (3) exited through the throat.[27] Each of these three points can be tested against the evidence.

1. **Entrance.** The decisive question here is: Was the entrance wound in the back above or below the "exit" wound in the throat? The Commission established that the bullet was traveling downward and was undeflected.[28] The entrance wound therefore had to be *above* the exit wound, i.e., at or above "throat" level. But the FBI Summary Report states that the bullet entered "just below his shoulder . . . at an angle of 45 to 60 degrees downward."[29] If this were the case, this bullet could not have exited from the throat.

The Warren Report states that the bullet entered the "rear of the neck," a position which would permit the bullet to exit through the throat wound.[30] Commander James J. Humes, the Navy pathologist who had conducted the autopsy and signed the Commission's autopsy report, testified that the conclusion that the bullet had exited was based mainly on the fact that "the wound in the anterior portion of the neck [was] physically lower than the point of entrance posteriorly."[31] Humes supported his assertion with two schematic drawings of the President—profile and back—which show the purported point of entry in the back of the neck (Commission Exhibit 385, on the next page, is one of these drawings). Although the artist who made these drawings was not familiar with the autopsy itself or photographs of it—he had made the drawings solely on the basis of the verbal instructions of Commander Humes[32]—these schematic drawings were offered

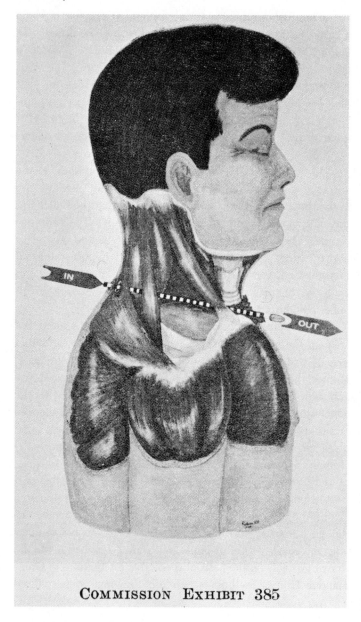

COMMISSION EXHIBIT 385

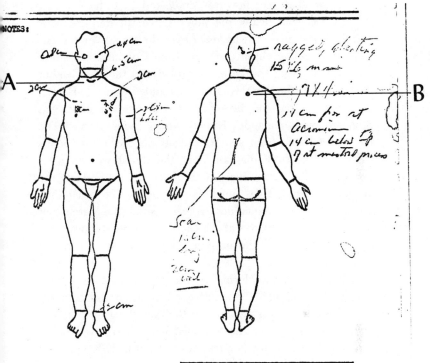

Pathologist

COMMISSION EXHIBIT 397

as evidence in lieu of the photographs and X-rays of the autopsy, which were "unavailable."[33]

Other evidence, however, indicated that the entrance wound was well below the point shown in the schematic drawings and, in fact, was *lower* than the throat wound. The face sheet of the autopsy report (from Commission Exhibit 397, see page 53; the letters A and B and the lines leading from them to the wounds have been added by me.—E.J.E.), which is not part of the official autopsy report itself, was prepared by Commander Humes *during* the autopsy.[34] The face sheet shows front and back diagrams of the President's body. On the front diagram (left) the throat wound (A) is just below the collar line; on the back diagram (right) the entrance wound (B) is much farther below the collar line. Thus, although Commander Humes testified in March that the entrance wound was above the throat wound, during the autopsy he marked the entrance wound below the throat wound.

It is possible that during the autopsy Commander Humes inaccurately marked the relative positions of the entrance wound and the throat wound on the face sheet, but there is further evidence that the entrance wound was well below the collar line. Secret Service Agent Clinton Hill, who was called into the autopsy examination for the express purpose of observing the position of the wounds, testified that he "saw an opening in the back, about six inches below the neckline. . . ."[35] Secret Service Agent Glen A. Bennett, who was in the car immediately behind the Presidential limousine, stated that he saw a "shot hit the President about four inches down from the right shoulder."[36] Two other Secret Service agents who were present at the autopsy repeatedly described the wound as a "shoulder" wound.[37]

Although this testimony is consistent with the FBI Summary Report's description of an entrance wound "just below his shoulder," and inconsistent with the Warren Report's description of a wound in the "rear of the neck," it is by no means conclusive. Human observations are often inaccurate, and it is possible that a coincidence of errors occurred.

However, there is more substantial evidence which fixes the position of the entrance wound. The FBI Supplemental Report includes photographs of the President's jacket and shirt which graphically show the entrance holes (FBI Exhibits 59 and 60, pages 56 and 57). These photographs, which were omitted from the Warren Report and the twenty-six volumes of supporting evidence,[38] show that the bullet hole in the jacket is 5 and ⅜ inches below the top of the collar and that the bullet hole in the shirt is 5 and ¾ inches below the top of the collar.[39] This position virtually coincides with the position shown in the face sheet of the autopsy report and with the FBI's description of the wound. It is, however, obviously inconsistent with the position of the entrance wound in the Commission's schematic drawings and with the wound described in the Commission's autopsy report.

It is possible that President Kennedy's jacket was in some manner raised more than six inches, so that the hole in it coincided with the purported entrance wound in the "back of the neck." (The Zapruder film, however, gives no indication of this.) It was, however, virtually impossible for the hole in the shirt (Exhibit 60) to have coincided with an entrance wound in the "back of the neck" (see Commission Exhibit 385, page 52). This could only have happened under either of the following two conditions: (1) the entire shirt, collar included, was raised almost six inches; or (2) a portion of the shirt was raised over the collar line (and thus doubled over). Obviously a *closed* shirt collar could not have been raised almost six inches on the neck, and therefore, for the shirt hole to have coincided with the purported entrance wound (which was above the collar line), the shirt would have to have been

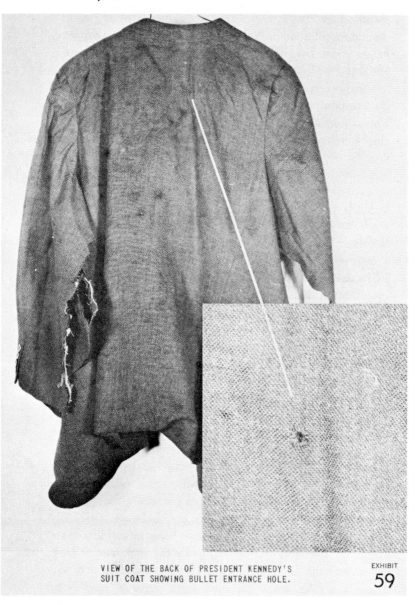

VIEW OF THE BACK OF PRESIDENT KENNEDY'S
SUIT COAT SHOWING BULLET ENTRANCE HOLE.

EXHIBIT
59

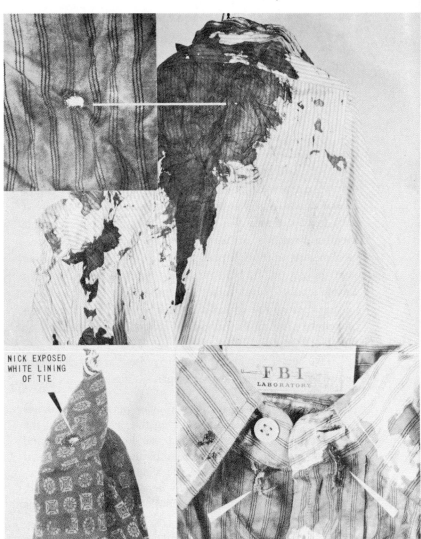

NICK EXPOSED
WHITE LINING
OF TIE

FBI
LABORATORY

VIEW OF THE BACK OF PRESIDENT KENNEDY'S SHIRT WITH CLOSE-UP
OF BULLET ENTRANCE HOLE. LOWER TWO PHOTOGRAPHS SHOW PRO-
JECTILE EXIT HOLE IN COLLAR AND NICK IN RIGHT SIDE OF TIE.

EXHIBIT
60

doubled-up over the collar. Since only one bullet hole was found in the back of the shirt, this could not have been the case.[40] Thus, according to the FBI photograph of the President's shirt, the bullet entrance hole in the President's back was *lower* than the throat wound. This is clearly inconsistent with the statement in the Commission's autopsy report.

2. Path. Did the bullet pass completely through the President's neck? The FBI Summary Report says that the autopsy revealed that it did *not*; the Warren Report claimed that the autopsy revealed that it did. It is a *sine qua non* law of forensic pathology that if a bullet passes through a body it must leave a discernible path.[41] Dr. Milton Helpern, Chief Medical Examiner of New York City and one of the foremost experts on forensic pathology, explained that "there is no such thing as a rifle bullet's passing through a neck without leaving a path."[42] Dr. Helpern estimated that a 6.5-mm. bullet passing through the President's neck would leave a track approximately ¼ inch in diameter.[43] Evidence indicates that no such track was found.

Two Secret Service agents were present at President Kennedy's autopsy. Agent Roy Kellerman testified:

> There were three gentlemen who performed this autopsy. A Colonel Finck—during the examination of the President, from the hole that was in his shoulder, and with a probe, and we were standing right alongside of him, he is probing inside the shoulder with his instrument and I said "Colonel, where did it go?" He said, "There are no lanes for an outlet of this entry in this man's shoulder."[44]

Lieutenant Colonel Pierre A. Finck is a nationally known expert on forensic pathology and wound ballistics. It is extremely unlikely that he would make such a definite statement if there could possibly have been a "lane for an outlet."[45]

Agent William Greer also testified that the autopsy doctors could not find a path for the bullet. One doctor told Greer that the bullet could very well have fallen out through the entrance wound if heart massage had been applied by the Dallas doctors.[46] When asked if "anything [was] said about any channel being present in the body for the bullet to have gone on through . . ." Greer replied:

No, sir; I hadn't heard anything like that, any trace of it going on through.[47]

Commander Humes testified that the autopsy doctors were unable "to take probes and have them satisfactorily fall through any path at this point."[48] Humes testified that he had not discerned a path for the bullet but had *deduced* its path from the entrance and the assumed exit wound, and from a slight bruise on the right lung.[49] Thus the autopsy surgeons were unable to find a path for the bullet.

Although the failure to find a path is consistent with the FBI Supplemental Report's statement that the bullet "penetrated to a distance of less than a finger length," it is inconsistent with the Warren Report's statement that the bullet passed through the President's body.

3. Exit Wound. The FBI Supplemental Report states that the autopsy revealed that the bullet did not exit from the President's body; and it implies that the throat wound was caused by a "projectile" from a third bullet that had hit the President's head.[50] The Warren Report states that the autopsy revealed that the bullet exited through the throat wound.

The throat wound, to be sure, was not seen by the autopsy surgeons because a tracheotomy operation, performed in Dallas immediately after the shooting, had obliterated the outlines of the wound. Only a few Dallas doctors actually observed the wound.[51] Dr. Malcolm Perry, who performed the tracheotomy, described the wound as a small puncture wound approximately 5 millimeters in diameter.[52] The bullet, however, was 6.55 millimeters in diameter; and the relatively small size of the wound suggested that it was caused by a fragment rather than a whole bullet.[53]

The Commission's version of the autopsy held that a *whole* bullet had exited from the throat.[54] However, the doctors who actually observed the throat wound specified that a whole bullet could have exited through the throat wound only under certain conditions. Dr. Ronald Jones testified that he thought that such a small throat wound could have been caused by a whole bullet only if it was traveling at an extremely low velocity, "to the point that you might think that this bullet barely made it through the soft tissues. . . ."[55] This would present a problem: a nearly spent bullet most probably could not have continued on to cause all Governor Connally's three wounds, and therefore it could not have been found on Connally's stretcher. Nor, if the bullet exited from President Kennedy's throat, was it probable that it was found on his stretcher. Yet a nearly whole bullet was found on one of the two stretchers in the Dallas hospital. It is possible that the bullet found on the stretcher came from the second shot, but this would necessarily mean that, if the first bullet to strike the President exited from his throat, it escaped the limousine and was never found. Thus, although it is possible that the throat wound was an exit wound for a whole bullet, the probability of this is severely diminished by other circumstances.

Furthermore, if accurate, the testimony of Secret Service Agent Roy Kellerman makes it extremely doubtful that the throat wound was caused by the first bullet to strike the President. Kellerman, who was in the front seat of the President's limousine, testified that he distinctly heard the President say, "My God, I am hit," *after* the first shot.[56] Since the projectile that caused the throat wound also punctured the windpipe, it is medically highly improbable that the President could speak *after* he received the throat wound.[57] This fact would be consistent with the FBI's version of the autopsy, which implies that the throat wound was caused by a fragment from a later bullet, but inconsistent with the Commission's version of the autopsy, which holds that the first bullet to hit the President exited from his throat.

Conclusion. The Warren Report and the FBI Summary and Supplemental Reports give diametrically opposed versions of the autopsy findings on the crucial question of whether or not the first bullet to hit the President exited from his throat. The Commission published an autopsy report that said it did; the FBI said that the autopsy revealed that the bullet "penetrated to a distance of less than a finger length" and did *not* exit from the front of the body. One of these documents changed a central fact of the assassination.

At the very least, the Commission failed to resolve an important contradiction. Although the Commission sent a questionnaire to the FBI which asked the FBI to explain other points in the FBI Summary and Supplemental Reports, no questions were asked about the FBI's version of the autopsy.[58] If the FBI Summary and Supplemental Reports were inaccurate, it was incumbent upon the Commission to explain how an error of this magnitude could have occurred.

The evidence, however, indicates that the FBI reports are not erroneous. The photograph of the President's shirt is in itself cogent evidence that the bullet entered the President's body below the collar line, which is consistent with the FBI Summary Report's description of a wound "just below his shoulder." It is inconsistent, however, with the Commission's description of a wound in "the rear of the neck." If a bullet fired from above the President entered six inches *below* the collar line and was undeflected, it is inconceivable that it exited through the throat. The fact that the autopsy surgeons were not able to find a path for the bullet is further evidence that the bullet did not pass completely through the President's body. And the evidence surrounding the exit wound, although not conclusive, strongly indicates that it was caused by a fragment from a subsequent bullet. If the FBI reports are accurate, then a central aspect of the autopsy was changed more than two months after the autopsy examination, and the autopsy report published in the Warren Report is not the original one. If this is in fact the case, the significance of this alteration of facts goes far beyond merely indicating that it was not physically possible for a lone assassin to have accomplished the assassination. It indicates that the conclusions of the Warren Report must be viewed as expressions of political truth.

PART TWO

The Investigation

4

The Limits of the Investigation

The Problem

THE CRITICAL PROBLEM in government investigations is inherent in the evaluation, not the accumulation, of data. The fact that the government can amass a virtually unlimited amount of information on any given subject only intensifies the problem. Each increment of data requires a proportionate increment of man-hours of reasoned judgment for evaluation. However, reasoned judgment is a limited commodity. This tends to be especially true in a government inquiry, because those men with sufficient authority to sit in judgment are almost invariably men occupied by other important responsibilities. The more important the inquiry, the more responsible the judges must be, and thus the more limited their available time. In a high-level inquiry the inevitable gap between the almost unlimited data and the extremely limited amount of evaluation time can be bridged only by a staff. The staff's function is to organize the data, sorting out the important from the unimportant facts, so that the data can be evaluated by the judges in the limited time available.

The Warren Commission probably represents an extreme example of this problem. The seven members of the Commission were all busy as well as eminent men whose time was severely limited by other pressing responsibilities. For example, Chief Justice Earl Warren had agreed to serve on the Commission only on the condition that it would not interfere with his work on the Court.[1] And the Supreme Court is one of the most time-consuming jobs in government; every brief must be read by each justice, and none of this work can be delegated. Thus, Warren could devote to Commission work only the time left after he had attended to his court duties. The other members, possibly to a lesser degree, had the same problem.

The amount of data the Commission received was truly prodigious; twenty-eight government agencies furnished more than three hundred cubic feet of paper. The FBI alone sent the Commission twenty-five thousand reports, which were mostly unindexed, unsummarized, and uncollated.[2] Quite obviously this mass of data had to be reduced to manageable proportions before the Commission could evaluate it.

The task of organizing and structuring the data was delegated to the legal staff. The Report stated:

As these investigative reports were received, the staff began analyzing and summarizing them. The members of the legal staff, divided into teams, proceeded to organize the facts revealed by these investigations, determine the issues, sort out the unresolved problems, and recommend additional investigation by the Commission.[3]

The staff not only organized the data for the Commission, it also was given the job of verifying the material and filling in the gaps. J. Lee Rankin, the General Counsel, said, "The lawyers *were* the independent investigators."[4] The lawyers took testimony from 418 witnesses, staged reconstructions, developed expert testimony, made inquiries to federal agencies about inconsistencies in their reports, and, in short, conducted the basic investigation and critical reassessment of the evidence for the Commission.

The Threshold Question

The threshold question for the Commission was: Was there more than one assassin? If Oswald acted alone, the investigation had no more to do than substantiate the case against him and explore his life history for possible motives. If, however, more than one person was involved in the assassination, the nature and scope of the investigation would have to be radically changed; new evidence and new hypotheses would have to be sought, new suspects found, new indictments rendered. Once across the threshold, the investigation would enter a new dimension of uncertainty; no one could know where it would lead, when it would end, or what would be its ramifications.

Was the investigation exhaustive not only in exploring Oswald's life history but also in searching for evidence of a second assassin? This question takes on crucial importance in light of the Zapruder film of the assassination and the FBI Summary and Supplemental Reports. It will be recalled that the film showed that President Kennedy and Governor Connally were hit almost simultaneously, and it was later established that the murder weapon could not be fired twice within this time period. The FBI reports precluded the possibility that both men were hit by the same bullet. There was thus a *prima facie* case of two assassins.

If there had been other evidence that precluded the possibility of a second assassin—for example, if all the bullets had been ballistically matched to the murder weapon—the Commission could reasonably have assumed that somehow the analysis of the film was fallacious. However, although the evidence identified Oswald as one assassin, it did not rule out the possibility of a second assassin. One bullet, which possibly was the fatal bullet, was too fragmented to be matched to Oswald's rifle by means of ballistics.[5] Thus the possibility of a second rifle existed. One identifiable but unidentified palm print was found on the "sniper's nest,"[6] and thus the possibility of an accomplice remained open. The fact that Oswald was able to escape from the murder scene suggested that a second assassin could also have escaped undetected.[7]

Recognizing the difficulty of proving a negative statement to a certainty, the Commission reasoned that if a conspiracy had existed some evidence of it doubtless would have come to the attention of the federal investigative agencies.[8] Since no such evidence had come to light, the Commission concluded explicitly "on the basis of evidence before the Commission" that "Oswald acted alone."[9]

This argument is compelling only if all pertinent evidence found by the federal agencies was, in fact, brought before the Commission. This, however, was not the case. For example, there was eyewitness evidence of a possible second assassin—evidence that never reached the Commission, despite the fact that it was submitted by the FBI.

The Neglected Eyewitness

On December 4, 1963, less than two weeks after the assassination, two FBI agents interviewed Mrs. Eric Walther, an eyewitness. She told them that she was standing across the street from the Texas Book Depository immediately before the assassination and that she saw a man with a rifle in an upper-story window of the building. She stated:

In his hands, this man was holding a rifle with the barrel pointed downward, and the man was looking south on Houston Street. The man was wearing a white shirt and had blond or light hair.

The FBI report continued:

The rifle had a short barrel and seemed large around the stock or end of the rifle. Her impression was that the gun was a machine gun. She noticed nothing like a telescopic sight on the rifle or a leather strap or a sling on the rifle. She said she knows nothing about rifles or guns of any type, but she thought the rifle was different from any she had ever seen. This man was standing in or about the middle of the window. In the same window, to the left of this man, she could see a portion of another man standing by the side of this man with a rifle. The other man was standing erect and his head was above the open portion of the window. As the window was very dirty, she could not see the head of the second man. She is positive that the window is not as high as the sixth floor. This second man was apparently wearing a brown suit coat, and the only thing she could see was the right side of the man, from about the waist to the shoulders. Almost immediately after noticing this man with the rifle and the other man standing beside him, someone in the crowd said "Here they come. . . ."[10]

Seconds later the Presidential motorcade passed Mrs. Walther, and she heard shots.[11]

What happened to Mrs. Walther's account? On December 5 FBI Report DL 89-43, containing Mrs. Walther's statement, was filed in Dallas.[12] It was submitted to the Commission on December 10 and became part of "Commission Document No. 7."[13] It was, however, never brought to the attention of the Commission. Mrs. Walther was not called as a witness. She was never questioned by the staff lawyers, and no requests were made for further FBI investigation of her statement.[14] In short, Mrs. Walther's account was never evaluated.

In view of the mass of investigative reports confronting the staff, it would be reasonable to expect that accounts containing major contradictions might be disregarded without further investigation. Mrs. Walther's account, however, contained no such contradictions. The fact that Mrs. Walther thought that the rifleman was on the fifth rather than on the sixth floor was a common mistake among witnesses.[15] The mistake stemmed from the fact that there were no windows on the ground floor of the book depository, and thus witnesses counting upward tended to mistake the sixth-floor window for the fifth-floor window.[16] Mrs. Walther's description of other details, such as the window and the rifleman's clothes, hair, and position, was consistent with the descriptions given by all other witnesses who saw a rifleman prior to the assassination.[17]

There was another witness who partially corroborated Mrs. Walther's statement—Arnold Rowland. Rowland, the only witness to identify the rifle correctly (as a rifle equipped with a telescopic sight) *before* it was found, testified that he had seen a rifleman in a sixth-floor window and that he had also seen a second person on the same floor.[18] The Commission rejected the latter part of Rowland's testimony partly because of "the lack of probative corroboration."[19]

If the staff had questioned Mrs. Walther it might have found that her statement was inaccurately transcribed by the FBI agents, that her eyesight was poor, or that she had an overactive imagination. On the other hand, it might have found that she knew further details to corroborate her story. The point is that, without having questioned Mrs. Walther, the Commission had no basis whatsoever for evaluating her eyewitness statement that a second man was standing next to the assassin. Yet, since the Commission stated categorically that none of the witnesses "testified to seeing more than one person in the window,"[20] quite obviously it failed to take Mrs. Walther's statement into account. A key question to understanding the workings of the Commission is: Why?

A Thorough and Massive Examination

Many critics of the Commission contend that the Commission controlled the investigation for its own purposes, that it carefully and purposefully selected witnesses who supported its preconceived findings and called no witnesses whose testimony might damage its case.

Such a view has the appeal of simplicity, but there is no evidence that the Commission, or even J. Lee Rankin, exerted detailed control over the investigation. The working papers of the staff show that they were free to call any witnesses they chose, and approval from Rankin was merely a formality.[21] Of the more than four hundred requests for witnesses whom the lawyers wished to interview, not one request was vetoed or denied.[22] All the lawyers interviewed emphatically agreed that the Commission played no part in the selection of their witnesses. Witnesses were selected from more than thirty thousand separate investigative reports, and there is no reason to believe that the Commission had the time or inclination to attempt to control this process. Thus there is no basis in fact for a conspiracy theory as to why certain witnesses were called and others were not.

The reason Mrs. Walther was never questioned by the Commission or staff, though less diabolical, is more revealing of the true nature of the investigation. She was not called, not because the Commission feared or suppressed her statement, but most probably because the staff overlooked it. If it is difficult to accept this explanation, that is only because of the common misconception that the Warren Commission's investigation was the most massive and thorough in history, and that no stone was left unturned in the quest for truth. This picture, painted so effusively by the mass media immediately following the release of the Warren Report,[23] was based not on analysis of the investigation but on faith in the individual members of the Commission.[24] It prevailed most probably because people wanted to believe that the investigation was exhaustive and thus that the doubts and uncertainties had been settled once and for all.

Rather than being "exhaustive," however, the Commission's investigation was actually an extremely superficial investigation limited in terms of both time and manpower, and consequently limited to the more prominent evidence. The limitations of the investigation can best be understood through an examination of its mechanics.

The Mechanics of the Investigation

It will be recalled that the legal staff was divided into six panels of lawyers; each panel consisted of a "senior" and "junior" lawyer; and each panel was assigned a specific area to investigate.

Only the first two panels, however, were directly concerned with the assassination itself. Panel I was assigned the task of establishing the basic facts of the assassination; its senior lawyer was Francis W. H. Adams, a former New York City police commissioner, and its junior lawyer was Arlen Specter, a young assistant district attorney from Philadelphia. Panel II was assigned the task of identifying the assassin; both its senior lawyer, Joseph Ball, and its junior lawyer, David Belin, had had extensive trial experience.

The four other panels were concerned with peripheral areas. Panel III interviewed Oswald's relatives and acquaintances, from his birth to his death, and attempted to reconstruct his life history. Panel IV investigated Oswald's movements outside the United States, and possible previous conspiratorial relationships involving Oswald. Panel V was concerned with Oswald's death and the actions of Jack Ruby. And Panel VI was assigned the area of "Presidential protection."

None of these peripheral panels would necessarily touch on the threshold question of a second assassin. Interviews with Oswald's acquaintances would cast light on the assassination itself only if those interviewed had known of the assassination in advance and were willing to admit it. As can be expected, however, none of the witnesses admitted any prior knowledge of the assassination. Thus, if the threshold question was to be answered, it would have to be answered by the first two panels.

The first limitation on the investigation was time. There was a June 1, 1964, deadline for the lawyers to make their investigation, interview witnesses, and submit their draft chapters.[25] The start of the investigation, however, was delayed until March 14 by the Ruby trial.[26] Thus only ten weeks actually remained for the investigation to be held.

The second limitation was manpower. Francis Adams, the senior lawyer assigned the task of ascertaining the basic facts, came to Washington only "a few days" during the entire investigation.[27] Rankin seriously considered asking for Adams' formal resignation, but as such an action might be misinterpreted as a sign of dissension among the staff, he decided to "leave Adams' name on the report."[28] Adams said that although he had a different concept of the investigation— he thought the FBI Summary and Supplemental Reports should have been verified immediately, so that the basic facts of the assassination could have been made public as soon as possible—the reason he left the Commission was that his law firm needed his services.[29] Whatever the reasons for Adams' de facto resignation, the full work load of Panel I devolved on Arlen Specter.

The fact that the lawyers were working as part-time consultants further complicated the problem. Joseph Ball, the senior lawyer on Panel II, was also a senior partner in a large California law firm, and he found it necessary to "commute" back and forth from California almost weekly.[30] Administrative assistant Howard Willens said, "The lawyers would fly back to Los Angeles or Des Moines between every assignment. That was no way to run an investigation. What we needed was forty law drones, fresh out of law school, not a handful of high-priced consultants."[31]

Area I: The Basic Facts

Instead of being handled by forty full-time lawyers, the entire task of ascertaining the basic facts of the assassination fell upon one lawyer—Arlen Specter. Specter had the responsibility for determining the source of the shots, the number of assassins, the exact manner in which the President and Governor Connally were shot, and the sequence of events[32]—in short, all the facts of the assassination.

Ascertaining facts is a time-consuming and arduous process. It is doubtful whether any one lawyer—or even any ten lawyers—could have established with precision in a ten-week period every fact involved in the assassination. Quite obviously, Specter had to be selective. He himself recognized this, commenting that he had to allocate most of his time to a limited number of major problems.[33]

Whereas a positive premise can be proved by establishing only the major facts, a negative premise can be proved only by establishing *all* the relevant facts, even the insignificant ones, and testing all the possibilities. Specter was faced with just such a negative premise: to prove that Oswald had had no assistance. The way in which he handled this problem indicates the extent to which the threshold question was approached.

Specter began his field investigation on March 16, 1964, with a specific assignment from the Chief Justice. Warren told Specter that it was of the utmost importance "to clear up the confusion" over Kennedy's throat wound.[34] One troublesome rumor was that the doctors in Dallas had identified the throat wound as an *entry* wound, and this suggested that Kennedy had been shot from the front. Specter asked when he should leave for Dallas, and Warren replied, "I'd hoped you could catch the evening plane tonight."[35]

Specter departed for Dallas that evening, and during the next eight days he interviewed, both "off-" and "on-the-record," twenty-eight doctors and other medical personnel at Parkland Hospital.[36] With one minor exception, these interviews comprised Specter's entire field investigation of "the basic facts of the assassination."[37]

Specter resolved the problem of the throat wound. All the doctors who saw the wound agreed that it could have been either an entry or an exit wound. Specter traced the rumor that it was an entrance wound to an answer Dr. Malcolm Perry had made to a hypothetical question. Dr. Perry admitted to Specter that he had no basis for telling whether it was an entrance or exit wound, and he testified that he had only said that it *could* have been an entrance wound.[38] Specter thus accomplished his mission and returned to Washington.

Quite obviously, if a lawyer was required to spend about two-thirds of his entire field investigation on a single problem, as Specter had to do, other problems had to be investigated with less thoroughness. Specter apparently preferred to allocate his limited time to problems that could be resolved instead of to problems that seemed unresolvable. This meant that a number of the more difficult problems were treated superficially. For example, the very important problem of where "bullet 399" was found was never resolved.

The Stretcher Bullet. Bullet 399 is a nearly intact bullet that ballistically was matched to the murder weapon. It was found on a stretcher at Parkland Hospital and turned over to the Secret Service. Although the question of whether it was found on President Kennedy's or Governor Connally's stretcher may have seemed insignificant at the time, it later assumed vital importance. If the bullet had come from Kennedy's stretcher it could not have passed through his body, and therefore Connally could only have been struck by a seprate bullet; thus the inescapable possibility of a second assassin was raised. On the other hand, if the bullet had come from Connally's stretcher, it would be consistent with the theory that both men were hit by the same bullet.

The question of where bullet 399 was found first arose at the March 16 Commission hearing, while Specter was questioning Commander James Humes, the autopsy surgeon. Allen Dulles was apparently under the impression that the bullet had been found on Kennedy's stretcher—a reasonable assumption in the light of the FBI Summary Report and Secret Service testimony.[39] Dulles asked if there had been further evidence on this question, and Specter replied:

> There has been other evidence, Mr. Dulles. If I may say at this point, we shall produce later, subject to sequential proof, evidence that the stretcher on which the bullet was found was the stretcher of Governor Connally.[40]

Specter, however, was being less than exact in his statement to Dulles. At this time Specter had not yet gone to Dallas, and all the FBI and Secret Service reports indicated that the bullet had *not* been found on Connally's stretcher.[41] Specter's assertion was apparently based not on the evidence, but on his expectation of what the evidence would show. Dulles then asked what happened to the first bullet that had hit Kennedy, and Specter replied, "That is the subject of some theories I am about to get into."[42]

Specter then developed the hypothesis that both men were wounded with the same bullet (bullet 399) and that therefore the bullet had been found on Connally's stretcher.[43]

Four days *after* Specter told the Commission that "the

evidence will show that it was from Governor Connally's stretcher that the bullet was found," he went to Dallas and questioned the witness who had actually found the bullet, Darrell Tomlinson.[44] Tomlinson, an engineer who was employed by the hospital, said that he thought that the bullet had *not* come from the stretcher identified as Connally's.[45] Despite a number of confusing questions put to him by Specter,[46] Tomlinson maintained that, although he was not "positively sure," he believed that the bullet had come from the stretcher parked in front of Connally's in the emergency room.[47] Thus Tomlinson provided evidence that contradicted the hypothesis Specter was committed to proving.

Specter said that he had "deductively proved" that the bullet had come from Connally's stretcher by precluding the possibility that the other stretcher was Kennedy's.[48] Two reasons were given for eliminating Kennedy's stretcher as the source of the bullet. First, Kennedy's stretcher was wheeled into "trauma room number 2" immediately after the body was removed from it. Second, two nurses said that the sheets were removed from Kennedy's stretcher; whereas Tomlinson claimed that there was a sheet on the foot of the stretcher from which the bullet had fallen.[49] Both these reasons were, however, extremely tenuous grounds for precluding Kennedy's stretcher.

The fact that Kennedy's stretcher was moved into trauma room number 2, which connected with the corridor in which the bullet was found, in no way precluded the possibility that the stretcher was later wheeled into this corridor. Since all stretchers were eventually returned to this area to be remade, the key question was: Was Kennedy's stretcher returned before or after the bullet was found? This question was never answered.[50]

The fact that two nurses recollected, four months after the event, that all the sheets were removed from Kennedy's stretcher hardly eliminated the stretcher as the source of the bullet. Also, Tomlinson's memory of a sheet on the foot of the stretcher could be inaccurate, or it was possible that, since the stretcher was parked near the linen hamper, a sheet could have been subsequently dropped on the stretcher.[51] Thus there was no credible reason for precluding the possibility that bullet 399 had come from Kennedy's stretcher.

There was, however, very definite evidence that precluded the possibility that bullet 399 had come from Connally's stretcher. Lieutenant Colonel Pierre A. Finck, the expert on forensic medicine, was asked if bullet 399 could have caused Connally's wrist wound. He replied flatly, "No, for the reason that there are too many fragments described in the wrist."[52] Since the Commission had established that all Connally's wrist and chest wounds had been caused by a single bullet, Colonel Finck's testimony excluded the possibility that bullet 399 had wounded Connally.[53] Therefore bullet 399 could not have passed through Connally and been found on his stretcher.

Colonel Finck's testimony on this point, which was fully supported by the other doctors,[54] cannot be dismissed merely because it collided with the hypothesis that bullet 399 was found on Connally's stretcher. Since Finck's categorical statement that this bullet could not have caused Connally's wrist wound was never challenged, disputed, or corrected, it can only be concluded from the evidence that bullet 399 did not come from Connally's stretcher.

The investigation of the stretcher bullet was by no means exhaustive. Two major witnesses were never questioned. After Tomlinson noticed the bullet, he called over the hospital's security director, O. P. Wright, who then picked up the bullet and turned it over to a Secret Service agent.[55] Wright very well might have been able to corroborate Tomlinson's story or to identify the stretcher that the bullet had come from, but he was never asked. Another witness who was never questioned was David Sanders, the orderly who wheeled Kennedy's stretcher out of the trauma room.[56] Sanders possibly could have answered the question of when Kennedy's stretcher arrived in the area in which the bullet was found.

An investigation in which expert testimony was ignored, two out of the three major witnesses were never questioned, and the working hypothesis was maintained despite the development of contradictory evidence can only be considered superficial. The case of the stretcher bullet illustrates the limits of the investigation; in ten days, or even in ten weeks, a single lawyer could not exhaust all the facts and possibilities in such a broad area as the "basic facts of the assassination." Arlen Specter spent only about ten days on his investigation in Dallas; quite obviously, he had to concentrate on the major problems and neglect some of the more minor ones.[57]

Specter said that he planned his investigation so that he could submit his chapter by the June 1 deadline, and he was, in fact, the only lawyer to meet this deadline.[58] As new evidence continued to develop after June 1, the premature termination of the investigation created a problem.

The Fourth Shot? At the time of the assassination a bystander, James Tague, was wounded by a minute fragment.[59] Although it is possible that this fragment came from one of the three established shots, it is also possible, especially in view of the distance involved, that the fragment came from a fourth shot. A fourth shot would not in itself indicate that a second assassin was at work—Oswald had sufficient time to fire a fourth shot after the fatal one—but it would cast new light on such problems as Connally's wrist wound, the dent in the chrome of the Presidential car, and the sequence of events. It would also raise a question as to why only three cartridge cases were found in the Texas Book Depository. In any case, the fourth hit on the curb was a basic fact of the assassination, and the way in which it was treated further illustrates the nature of the investigation.

Immediately after the assassination a number of witnesses reported that a bullet had struck the pavement and a bystander had been slightly wounded by the ricochet.[60] On January 11 these reports were submitted to the Commission by the Texas Attorney General and, in the parceling out of the investigative reports, these reports were sent to Specter's panel.[61]

In February, Specter apparently asked the Secret Service field office in Dallas to investigate the matter. The special agent in charge, Forrest Sorrels, reported that no bullet mark could be found on the pavement, and he added, "I did not see how it could have been possible for any fragment of any of the three bullets that were fired to have hit this concrete slab."[62] No further effort was made at the time to find the person who was hit by a fragment or to locate the bullet mark.

There was, however, a photograph of the bullet mark which failed to reach Specter's attention because of the "division of labor." Tom Dillard, a Dallas newspaper reporter, reported to the FBI that he had taken a photograph of the bullet mark. The FBI report of the Dillard interview was passed on to Ball's panel because it dealt primarily with the identification of the assassin.[63] Although Ball questioned Dillard, he apparently didn't realize the relevance of the Dillard photograph, and thus the information did not reach Specter's panel until after Specter had finished his investigation.[64]

In July the Dillard photograph finally was forwarded to the Commission.[65] Rankin immediately requested the FBI to locate the bullet mark, and he sent Wesley Liebeler, the junior lawyer on Panel III, to Dallas to interview James Tague, the bystander.[66] Tague told Liebeler that he had received a minor cut on his face after the second or third shot, and immediately afterward he and a deputy sheriff had located the bullet mark.[67] Liebeler then interviewed the deputy sheriff, who corroborated Tague's account.[68]

In August the FBI established through spectrographic analysis that a bullet fragment had definitely struck the curb about 260 feet from the President's car at the time of the third shot.[69] Thus, while the final draft of the Report was being written, the FBI laboratory confirmed that the mark on the curb had been caused by a bullet fragment.[70]

However, the chapter on the basic facts of the assassination had already been written, and at this late date there was apparently no interest in reopening the investigation.[71] Instead, a paragraph was inserted in the report, stating:

> . . . the mark on the south curb of Main Street cannot be identified conclusively with any of the three shots fired. Under the circumstances it might have come from the bullet which hit the President's head, or it might have been the product of the fragmentation of the missed shot upon hitting some other object in the area.[72]

The report failed to admit that the mark also might have come from a fourth shot.

An exhaustive investigation would have tested each of these three possibilities against the known facts. Was it ballistically possible for fragments from the head shot to travel 260 feet and strike the curb with sufficient kinetic energy then to strike Tague? Ballistics experts could have been called to testify on the probability of this happening. Did a shot, in fact, miss? The Commission did not reach a conclusion on this point; thus further testimony might have been called for. If these two possibilities were precluded, then a fourth shot must have been fired.

The reason why the problem of the fourth hit was not dealt with by the investigation was, quite simply, that mention of this hit was lost in the shuffle of investigative reports, and it did not come to light until after Specter had completed his investigation. This occurrence suggests that possibly other facts came to light after the June 1 deadline or were "lost in the shuffle."[73]

Thus the investigation in Area I, the "basic facts of the assassination," tended to be limited to the more prominent problems. There was neither time nor manpower to explore problems of a more nebulous nature. Consequently, while known facts were substantiated, unknown facts were left unknown.

Area II

The investigation of Area I was, to some degree, supplemented by the investigation of Area II, "the identity of the assassin." There was, however, an important conceptual difference between the two investigations: whereas the first investigation was charged with ascertaining *all* the basic facts of the assassination and therefore had to be exhaustive in scope, the second investigation was charged with establishing a single positive fact, the identity of the assassin.

Joseph Ball, the most experienced trial lawyer on the staff, said that his investigation of Area II required basically the same process that a lawyer uses in "building a case"; a chain of evidence had to be forged which indisputably linked Oswald to the assassination and also showed that Oswald had the opportunity to commit the act.[74] Ball thus had a very definite, and limited, objective.

First Ball and his junior lawyer, David Belin, reviewed the investigative reports and isolated the "chain of evidence." Ball then prepared a "Harvard outline" of his case, in which each major element of evidence was supported by the minor and circumstantial evidence. From this outline Ball determined the facts that required further investigation and the evidence that required substantiation.[75]

After the Ruby trial ended, Ball and Belin began their field investigation in Dallas. Most of the key witnesses were interviewed informally, and on March 20 Ball held an "off-the-record" reconstruction of the assassin's movements. The purpose of this reconstruction was to prove that Oswald had had the opportunity to commit the assassination and then escape.[76]

The first question dealt with was how Oswald had descended from the sixth to the second floor undetected. Three witnesses on the fifth floor had indicated to the FBI that they had had a view of the stairs after the assassination and that no one had gone down them.[77] This at first led to the theory that Oswald had used the elevator, but this proved impossible because both elevators were found on the fifth floor with their doors open immediately after the assassination.[78] In the re-enactment Ball determined that the three witnesses, in fact, could not have seen the staircase at all times, and thus it was possible for Oswald to have descended the stairs undetected.[79]

Since a policeman had encountered Oswald on the second floor shortly after the last shot was fired, there was also a question of time. Could Oswald have descended from the sixth to the second floor in the time it took the policeman to rush up to the second floor? In the reconstruction, Ball clocked both the assassin's and the policeman's movements with a stopwatch and thereby showed that it was possible for Oswald to have been the assassin.[80]

To prove that Oswald was the assassin, Ball relied mainly on scientific evidence. This "hard" evidence was judiciously and methodically developed by Melvin Eisenberg before the Commission itself. The chain of evidence was indeed compelling.

Bullet fragments found in the President's car were definitely matched by ballistics experts to the rifle found in the Texas Book Depository. The rifle was traced to Oswald, and handwriting experts helped confirm that Oswald had ordered and paid for the gun. In addition, fingerprint experts identified as Oswald's a palm print taken from the rifle, and thus it was established that Oswald had had possession of the rifle. In short, the chain of evidence indisputably showed that Oswald's rifle was used in the assassination.[81]

The fact that Oswald had the opportunity to be the assassin and the fact that his rifle was used in the assassination in themselves made a *prima facie* case for Oswald's involvement in the assassination. Although the possibility that Oswald was unwittingly involved (that is, "framed") was apparently not explored, other circumstances—such as the shooting of police officer J. D. Tippit—severely diminished the credibility of this possibility.

Although the Area II investigation fulfilled, with reasonable thoroughness, its mission of identifying Oswald as the assassin, it tended to disregard possible evidence of accomplices. For example, Ball cited Oswald's palm prints on the book cartons used by the assassin as evidence that Oswald was at the scene of the assassination.[82] However, other unidentified palm prints were found on these cartons, which could have indicated the presence of an accomplice.[83] Ball and Belin did not try to have these prints identified, and it was only at the insistence of Wesley Liebeler, in August, that the FBI identified most, but not all, of the other identifiable prints.[84] Quite possibly Ball felt that the question of accomplices fell outside his investigation's purview of identifying the assassin. In any case, the Area II investigation focused on the positive evidence that identified Oswald as the assassin; it did not deal with the threshold question of a second assassin.

The Grassy Knoll

There were also problems that fell between Area I and Area II, and were not dealt with by either investigation. A case in point is "the grassy knoll." In March, Ball was asked by Warren to clear up a rumor that the shots had come from the railroad bridge over the triple underpass the President's car was approaching.[85] Ball, assisted by other lawyers, questioned witnesses who were standing on the railroad overpass at the time of the assassination, and the rumor proved baseless. However, six out of seven of these witnesses who gave an opinion as to the source of the shots indicated that the shots had come from a "grassy knoll" located between the overpass and the Texas Book Depository.[86] Echoes often cause misleading impressions as to the source of shots, but five of the witnesses on the overpass said that they had also seen smoke rise from the knoll area.[87] For example, one witness testified, "I definitely saw the puff of smoke and heard the report from under these trees [on the knoll]."[88]

The grassy knoll, however, did not fall within the bounds of Area II, and Ball and Belin did not question the witnesses who were standing on the knoll. And Specter apparently did not have time to attack this problem. Yet, according to the investigative reports, of the ten witnesses who were standing between the knoll and the President's car, and who had expressed an opinion as to the source of the shots, nine thought the shots had come from the knoll directly behind them, and the tenth thought the shots had come from the area between the knoll and the Book Depository.[89] Only one of these witnesses, Abraham Zapruder, was questioned by the staff, and he was called to determine not the source of the shots, but the terms under which he had sold his film of the assassination to *Life* magazine.[90]

Eight witnesses were standing across the street from the knoll; all eight said they thought the shots had come from the knoll.[91] Only three of these witnesses were questioned. Jean Hill was questioned by Specter after Mark Lane had described her account in his testimony before the Commission.[92] James Altgens was questioned by Liebeler primarily about a photograph that he had taken showing a person resembling Oswald in the doorway of the Texas Book Depository. And James Tague was questioned by Liebeler about the "fourth hit."[93]

Despite the fact that almost all the witnesses on the knoll, or with a view of the knoll, who expressed an opinion as to the source of the shots said that the shots had come from the knoll, no thorough investigation was made of this area. Very few of the witnesses who thought the shots had come from the knoll were questioned, and no full examination was made of photographs of the knoll area for indications of a second assassin.

If there was no evidence of more than one assassin, there was also no evidence that precluded the possibility. The conclusion that "Oswald acted alone" was predicated on two assumptions: first, that all the pertinent evidence was brought *before* the Commission for its evaluation; and second, that the staff's investigation had tested all possibilities after making an exhaustive analysis of all evidence and reports that might possibly have indicated the presence of a second assassin.

However, all the pertinent evidence was *not* brought before the Commission or even evaluated by the staff—as was the case with Mrs. Walther's statement. Nor did the staff conduct an exhaustive investigation into the basic facts of the assassination. In fact, only the more prominent problems were investigated, and many of the crucial, albeit less salient, problems were left unresolved—as was the case with the stretcher bullet. Furthermore, problems that developed after the deadline, such as the fourth hit, were never completely investigated. And although the investigation clearly delineated the chain of evidence linking Oswald to the assassination, it disregarded possible evidence of an accomplice in its handling of testimony involving the grassy knoll.

The investigation of the threshold question was thus a limited and relatively superficial one which never pursued answers to many important problems.

5

The Limits of the Investigators

THE COMMISSION conducted an independent investigation without independent investigators. The Commission found it unnecessary "to employ investigators other than the members of the Commission's legal staff," because it felt that it could rely on the facilities and investigative reports of the FBI and other federal agencies.[1] Although the Commission in fact relied mainly on the FBI, the investigation in theory was independent, because the legal staff "critically reassessed" the reports and work of the FBI and conducted further investigations where necessary.[2] J. Lee Rankin said, "Our lawyers were the only independent investigators that we needed."[3]

The legal staff thus had a dual role; it was the Commission's "independent investigator" as well as its counsel. In its investigative role, the staff was expected to analyze all the FBI reports for inconsistencies and gaps, and then to investigate and resolve these problems. In its legal role, the staff was expected to develop testimony and to examine witnesses before the Commission. In performing this dual function, however, the "independent investigators" were confronted with three problems that tended to limit the effectiveness of their investigation.

Communications with the FBI

Although the Commission borrowed lawyers from the Department of Justice, accountants from the Internal Revenue Service, and historians from the Department of Defense, it did not include FBI or other investigative agents on its staff.[4] One staff member wrote that this "initial organizational weakness" was probably due to "an early sensitivity to public opinion in view of rumors that Lee Harvey Oswald had a prior connection with the FBI."[5] In any case, the staff was effectively separated from the agents on whom it depended for its information.

Instead of having direct access to the FBI agents, the lawyers had to make each separate request for information and assistance through "channels." For example, Joseph Ball said that on his first trip to Dallas he called the FBI field office for assistance in a problem. He was told that the request must come from FBI headquarters in Washington. It was thus necessary for Ball to telephone Howard Willens in Washington, who then prepared a formal request which was, in turn, signed by J. Lee Rankin and forwarded to J. Edgar Hoover. Three days later Ball was notified by the Dallas field office that his request had been approved, but by this time Ball had resolved the problem and was ready to return to Washington. Ball added that the FBI was "exasperatingly bureaucratic."[6]

Rankin said that although there were some "communication problems" between the staff and the FBI, there was a liaison officer, Inspector James R. Malley, on whom he could call at "any time of the day or night" to expedite important problems.[7] Melvin Eisenberg said that although relations gradually improved, and eventually became good, FBI agents were initially resentful of "amateurs" doing what they considered to be their job.[8]

Other lawyers, however, were less satisfied with FBI cooperation. Joseph Ball said that FBI agents cooperated only on "express orders" from Hoover.[9] Wesley Liebeler said that, although the FBI was extremely efficient in answering questions submitted in writing, the agents would not develop any information that was not specifically requested of them.[10]

The practice of adhering to specific questions is probably the only way for an organization which conducts hundreds of thousands of interviews a year to function efficiently, but in the case of the Commission this method also had the effect of restricting the investigation to the more protrusive facts. For example, one witness, Arnold L. Rowland, testified before the Commission that he had told the FBI agents who interviewed him of a second person on the same floor as the rifleman a few minutes prior to the assassination. Rowland indicated that the FBI agents lacked interest in this second person.[11] He stated:

> . . . the agents were trying to find out if I could positively identify the man that I saw. They were concerned mainly with this, and I brought up to them about the Negro man [the second person] after I had signed the statement, and at the time they just told me that they were trying to find out about or if anyone could identify the man who was up there. They just didn't seem interested at all [in the other person]. They didn't pursue the point. They didn't take it down in notation as such.[12]

Rowland's account never appeared in any FBI report to the Commission.[13] Since Rowland had told deputy sheriff Roger Craig of a second person on the same floor with the assassin immediately after the assassination,[14] it seems probable that he would repeat the same story to FBI agents who interviewed him (as he claimed to have done), even if the story were not accurate. If Rowland did tell this story to the FBI, then FBI agents disregarded a very significant statement because it was not immediately relevant to their specific question. This possibility suggests that the FBI interviewing system was more effective in clarifying and verifying known information than it was in discovering and reporting new information.

Because of the enormous quantity of FBI reports the staff initially assumed that the FBI had carried out exhaustive research in the areas of its main investigation. Liebeler, however, later found that "the most disquieting thing about the FBI investigation was that it was less thorough than it appeared to be."[15] For example, although Marina Oswald had been repeatedly questioned and continually investigated over a nine-month period by the FBI, Liebeler found in August that she still possessed evidence, which had an important bearing on Oswald's trip to Mexico, that had never been brought to the attention of the Commission.[16]

Liebeler thus wrote a memorandum to Howard Willens, stating:

> . . . it reflects badly [on the thoroughness of the investigation] that Marina Oswald still had material on August 26 [1964] not known to the FBI.[17]

Thus the quantity of the FBI's investigative material did not guarantee that all the important facts were reported. In fact, the plethora of unevaluated FBI material probably added to the problem of critical reassessment. One staff lawyer estimated that 90 per cent of these reports were not immediately relevant to the assassination.[18]

The high proportion of irrelevant papers was caused in part by the FBI's policy of submitting reports on all the crank letters and "weird allegations" received by FBI field offices. J. Edgar Hoover explained that, even when an allegation could not possibly have a basis in fact, a report on it was submitted to the Commission "for the record."[19] One FBI document, the five-volume Gemberling Report, is over 1200 pages long, and even contains descriptions of dreams that persons had had after the assassination.[20]

Furthermore, the FBI system of investigating all names mentioned (they were capitalized in agents' reports, listed alphabetically by the field office, then circulated for further investigation to other field offices) produced thousands of pages on people who were only remotely connected with Oswald. Somewhat like a chain-letter in effect, this process produced investigations of and reports on acquaintances of acquaintances of acquaintances of Oswald.[21]

No single member of the staff was able to read all the FBI reports, and therefore no one had a synoptic view of the FBI investigation. The quantity of FBI reports thus may have had the unintended effect of obscuring relevant information.

The staff had only very limited assistance from the Central Intelligence Agency. Wesley Liebeler was one of the few staff lawyers who had direct contact with CIA agents; his experience illustrates the general problem "outsiders" (as the lawyers were considered to be) encountered in dealing with a highly secret intelligence organization. Liebeler, in attempting to identify a heavy-set man in a CIA photograph, found that the photograph itself had a curious history. On November 18, 1963, the FBI received it, together with a report on Oswald's

September 27, 1963, visit to the Cuban Embassy in Mexico City, and forwarded both to its Dallas field office. Coincidentally, the file arrived in Dallas on November 22, the day of the assassination. The following day FBI agent Bardwell Odum showed the photograph to Oswald's mother, who later alleged that it was a picture of Jack Ruby. To show that Mrs. Oswald was mistaken, the photograph was introduced into the record as "Odum Exhibit 1." Later Liebeler found that three different witnesses' descriptions of an unidentified associate of Oswald's seemed to resemble the man in the photograph.

Liebeler therefore asked the FBI to identify the man. The FBI replied that it was a CIA photograph, taken outside the country, and that they had no further information about it. Liebeler next wrote to the CIA, asking who the person in the photograph was and why it was sent to the FBI less than a week before the assassination. Weeks later the CIA still had not replied, and Liebeler consulted the CIA liaison with the Commission, R. G. Rocca, who told him that the matter was still being investigated. Later a CIA agent called Liebeler and said that the CIA had thought at the time the photograph was sent to the FBI that the person in the photograph was Lee Harvey Oswald. He explained that it was routinely taken on September 27 by a secret camera located across the street from the Cuban Embassy in Mexico City, and that the person was identified by a confidential source in the Embassy as Lee Harvey Oswald. And so the photograph was included with the report on Oswald. When Liebeler pointed out that the person did not resemble Oswald at all, the CIA agent said that he would investigate further and call back. Despite persistent inquiries, Liebeler heard nothing more about the man in the photograph, and he was not even able to get hold of the agent who had called him. Liebeler added that the CIA was so secretive that it was virtually useless to the Commission.[22]

In all, the CIA submitted only about forty-five reports, and these pertained mainly to investigations conducted abroad and to foreign newspaper reports.[23]

The Secret Service provided agents for specific assignments, though it had neither the manpower nor the facilities to conduct a general investigation.[24] In the final analysis, the staff was thus mainly dependent on the FBI for its information.

Although the FBI conducted a massive investigation— over 25,000 interviews and reinterviews—into the assassination and into the backgrounds of the principal persons involved, the communications problem between the staff and the FBI, and the narrow criteria of the interviews, served to restrict the flow of information to the more salient facts.

The Forensic Problem

The Commission required that all its processes be consistent with the "high judicial standards of its members."[25] This requirement led to the fair and judicial treatment of witnesses, but it also had the unintended effect of restricting the depth of the staff's investigation.

Forensic interrogation is the lawyer's only means of extracting concealed information from a witness; it includes such tactics as cross-examination, trap-questioning, and badgering. The Commission felt that, although these tactics might have a place in adversary proceedings where witnesses have interests to protect, they had no place in the proceedings of the Commission.[26] Since most of the witnesses appeared before the Commission voluntarily and without counsel, the

Commission believed that they should not be subject to rigorous cross-examination unless it was evident that they were concealing information.[27] The conflict between the staff's interest in interrogating witnesses and the Commission's interest in assuring that the proceedings were "a model of judicial fairness"[28] became evident after the first witness, Marina Oswald, testified.

Most of the lawyers were not satisfied with Mrs. Oswald's testimony. Liebeler said that it contained obvious contradictions and inconsistencies, and it seemed she might very well be "approximating the truth" in order to tell the Commission what she thought it wanted to hear.[29] Joseph Ball said that Marina Oswald "left too many questions unanswered."[30] William Coleman asked Rankin to permit Mrs. Oswald to undergo a more rigorous examination, and he reportedly offered to prepare a "trappy deposition" for her.[31]

At the next staff meeting Rankin announced that the Commission had decided against further examination of Marina Oswald. He went on to say that the Chief Justice considered himself to be "a judge of human beings" and he and the other Commissioners fully believed her testimony.[32]

The staff strongly and loudly protested this decision. Coleman threatened to resign unless Mrs. Oswald was examined further, and other lawyers came close to walking out of the meeting. Liebeler asked Rankin for the Commission's objection to further examination, and Rankin replied, "The Chief [Justice] doesn't want it." At this point Rankin lost control of the meeting.[33]

In a memorandum which possibly reflects the intensity of feeling on the subject, Norman Redlich alleged that

> Marina Oswald has lied to the Secret Service, the FBI, and this Commission repeatedly on matters which are of

vital concern to the people of this country and the world.[34]

Because of the Commission's insistence on "believing Marina," some members of the staff referred to the Commission as "Snow White and the Seven Dwarfs"—Marina Oswald being Snow White.[35]

The Commission finally relented and allowed further examination of Marina Oswald. She was called as the final Commission witness in September, and she changed an important part of her testimony—Oswald's motive. Whereas in February Mrs. Oswald said she had thought that the motive was fame, she said in September that she had always believed that Oswald was aiming at Governor Connally and not at the President.[36] More than one tenth of the time spent in Commission hearings was devoted to the testimony of Marina Oswald; yet the discrepancies in Mrs. Oswald's testimony were never satisfactorily resolved.

This case illustrates the difficulty the staff had in examining witnesses without being permitted to use the tools of forensic interrogation.

Lawyers taking testimony in their field investigations also were restricted in their treatment of witnesses. For example, one staff lawyer, Burt Griffin, was reprimanded for "using too much discretion."[37]

Griffin had been questioning Dallas police sergeant Patrick Dean about Ruby's entry into the basement of the Dallas city jail, and he found Dean's answers to be inconsistent with his earlier statements and with other evidence as well.[38] In an effort to clarify Dean's statements, Griffin went "off-the-record," sent the stenographer out of the room, and spoke to Dean informally for about twenty minutes.[39] According to Dean, Griffin had bluntly told him that he (Dean) was lying and had offered to help him keep his job if he told the truth.[40] When Dean complained of this treatment to the Commission, Chief Justice Warren stated:

> That so far as the jurisdiction of this Commission is concerned and its procedures, no member of our staff has a right to tell any witness that he is lying or that he is testifying falsely. That is not his business. It is the business of this Commission to appraise the testimony of all the witnesses. . . .[41]

Thus the staff was explicitly prohibited from controverting the testimony of witnesses. Although this was done to protect the rights of the witnesses, it had the effect of depriving the staff of a useful forensic tactic. Without the right to challenge witnesses with other evidence, some of the lawyers felt that "they were reduced to deposition-takers."[42]

The Commission's policy, that the staff's methods had to be consistent with the standards of the Commissioners, also limited the use of such quasi-legal devices as polygraph tests. Rankin said that the "Chief Justice could not give his seal of approval to devices that the courts have ruled illegal."[43]

A polygraph is not, as it is sometimes called, a "lie detector." It only measures emotional stress in a witness that *may* indicate deception or that may indicate other emotions such as fear, anxiety, nervousness, etc.[44] The results of a polygraph test depend largely on the subjective interpretation of the witness's responses and are thus of dubious value in determining the truthfulness of a witness.[45] Nevertheless, polygraphs have considerable value as investigative aids in certain circumstances. For example, if a witness believes that the instrument is in fact a "lie detector," it may provide a strong psychological inducement for him to be truthful.

Although the staff fully realized the limits of the polygraph test, some of the lawyers felt it was the only way to resolve certain problems.[46] For example, Liebeler was confronted with the testimony of a Dallas gunsmith, Dial D. Ryder, which, if true, would indicate that an important part of Oswald's life was unknown to the Commission.[47] Ryder claimed that the day after the assassination he had found a repair ticket for a rifle with the name "Oswald" on it. It was evident from the information on the repair ticket that this rifle could not have been the assassination weapon, and Ryder was certain that he had never worked on a rifle similar to the assassination weapon.[48] Since the FBI was unable to locate any other "Oswald" in the area who might have brought the rifle to Ryder, and since Oswald lived in the same neighborhood as the gun-repair shop, it seemed quite possible that Oswald owned a second rifle.

Two other witnesses testified that Oswald had inquired in a furniture store about having his rifle repaired. This occurred at about the same time that Ryder remembered repairing the rifle, and the witnesses also claimed that they had directed Oswald to Ryder's gun shop.[49] When Liebeler confronted the witnesses with Marina Oswald, both positively identified her as the woman who had entered the furniture store with Oswald.[50] There remained, however, the distinct possibility that the repair tag was spurious and that Ryder had invented the story.

In this situation, Liebeler felt that a "lie detector" probably would have induced Ryder to be truthful.[51] Furthermore, if the polygraph showed no emotional stress on Ryder's part, it would strongly suggest that Oswald's life was still a mystery and that further and more coercive questioning of Marina Oswald was called for. Liebeler said that the problem came down to: Was Ryder lying?[52]

In reply to Liebeler's request for an FBI polygraph test of Ryder, Willens wrote that "the FBI is extremely dubious of polygraphs" and that the Commission had therefore denied the request.[53] The problem of Oswald's "second rifle" thus was never resolved.

The staff's role of "independent investigator" was thus, to some degree, hampered by its role of "Commission counsel." Admittedly, as Eisenberg pointed out, this limitation affected only a very minor portion of the investigation.[54] Most of the witnesses came forth of their own accord and testified freely, and there was no need to subject them to rigorous cross-examination and quasi-legal tactics. There were, however, some problems that could not be resolved by merely accepting witnesses' testimony at face value and probing no further. Naturally a witness would be unlikely to reveal information indicating that he had prior knowledge of the assassination. Concealed information of this nature could have been elicited only through forensic interrogation. By denying the lawyers the use of these tactics, the Commission, in effect, limited the depth of the investigation to information that witnesses were willing to reveal openly.[55]

The Time-Pressure Problem

The third major problem that limited the lawyers in their investigation was time pressure. The constant deadlines limited not only the quantity of the investigation but also its quality.

As the investigation progressed into June, and the Commission was forced to extend the June 1 deadline to July 1, the Commissioners became increasingly anxious to terminate the investigation and to "get the report out."[56] John J. McCloy said that he was concerned with the "ugly rumors" that were circulating in Europe, and he feared that a delay in publishing the Report would "cause them to spread like wildfire."[57]

The Congressional members of the Commission felt it was necessary to release the Report well before the election.[58]

Whatever the exact reasons, considerable pressure was exerted on the lawyers through Rankin to "close down their investigations and submit their chapters."[59] To do so, lawyers, in some instances, were forced to leave important problems unresolved.

For example, Burt Griffin had the problem of determining how Ruby gained entrance to the basement of the Dallas city jail a few minutes before he murdered Oswald. The task was complicated by the fact that there were over one hundred witnesses in the basement at the time, and there were at least six different possible entranceways.[60] To scrutinize the statements of all these witnesses and to eliminate as possibilities some of the entranceways required a methodical approach and a great deal of time.

During his field investigation, Griffin found that Ruby's story that he had entered by the Main Street ramp was contradicted by other evidence. The police officer guarding the ramp categorically denied that Ruby could have entered by that ramp, and four police officers, who had driven up the ramp at virtually the only time that Ruby could have descended, testified that they did not see Ruby on the ramp.[61] This contradiction raised questions both about Ruby's truthfulness and about the possibility that he had had assistance in entering the basement.

In June the Commission reportedly felt that Griffin was spending too much time on this problem. Consequently, Griffin was ordered to proceed with other areas of his investigation, despite his protests that the question of Ruby's entrance was of prime importance.[62]

Thus the question was left unanswered, and the Report could only conclude: "Ruby entered the basement, unaided, probably via the Main Street ramp. . . ."[63]

Time pressure also forced the lawyers to attempt to preclude possibilities by means of tenuous deductive reasoning
rather than by further investigations. In some cases this
method led to premature conclusions.

For example, one witness, Sylvia Odio, gave testimony
indicating that Oswald had visited her in the company of two
"Cuban underground fighters" the day before he left on his
trip to Mexico. Mrs. Odio claimed that the man who was introduced to her as "Leon Oswald" was in fact Lee Harvey Oswald, and her sister corroborated this identification.[64]

If Mrs. Odio's testimony was accurate, it had important
implications for the investigation; it meant that Oswald had
two associates, not known to the Commission, who were involved in his trip to Mexico not long before the assassination.

By July the staff still had not questioned Sylvia Odio.
Meanwhile, W. David Slawson, the lawyer assigned to the
problem, tried to preclude the possibility of truth in Mrs.
Odio's story by showing that it was not possible for Oswald
to have been in Dallas at the time she claimed. Slawson's
analysis was based on the fact that Oswald was in New Orleans
at 8 a.m. on September 25 and on the bus bound from Houston
to Mexico at 6 a.m. on September 26. Slawson assumed that
Oswald had traveled from New Orleans to Houston on September 25 and then had caught the 2:35 a.m. bus to Mexico
the next morning. This left only a few hours unaccounted for
in Houston and "precluded" the possibility that Oswald had
visited Mrs. Odio in Dallas on September 25.[65]

Although the Commission decided, on the basis of this
analysis, that Mrs. Odio's story was false and required no
further investigation, Liebeler found that a number of details
in the woman's story coincided with facts she could not possibly have known, and he gave the matter further attention.
On investigating the bus schedules, he found that there was

no reason to assume that Oswald had caught the bus at 2:35 a.m. in Houston. Actually, Oswald was not seen on that bus until 6 a.m. that day. Thus Liebeler found it possible for Oswald to have traveled from New Orleans to Dallas on September 25, visited Mrs. Odio, and then continued to Alice, Texas, where he could have caught the Houston-to-Mexico bus. Mrs. Odio's story that Oswald had left her home in Dallas in an automobile with two other men thus could not, in fact, be ruled out.[66]

When Liebeler submitted a memorandum to Rankin showing the fallacy in the earlier analysis, Rankin said, "At this stage, we are supposed to be closing doors, not opening them."[67] Once the memorandum had been submitted, however, Rankin did give the matter further consideration, although the issue was never resolved.[68]

In this case a question which had been prematurely foreclosed was reopened through the persistence of a lawyer in another area. Indeed, other questions may have been closed by fallacious analyses and never reopened. The atmosphere of "closing doors" certainly was not conducive to critical re-examinations of the evidence.

The "independent investigators" were thus constrained in their investigation by the communications problem with the FBI, the forensic problem caused by the Commission's judicial requisites, and the time-pressure problem. Although these three problems limited to some degree the depth of the investigation, the question remains: How decisive were these limitations?

Despite the restricted flow of information from the FBI, the staff had virtually all its questions answered by the FBI. Despite the judicial restraints, most of the witnesses testified freely and only a small number of questions were left unanswered. Despite the time pressure, most of the salient problems were resolved. The only type of information unlikely to emerge in such an investigation would be information that was deliberately concealed.

The answer as to how decisive the limitation was, therefore, depends on whether or not information was concealed—a question which could not be answered by this type of investigation.

6

The Commission Hearings

THE STAFF INVESTIGATION was supplemented to some degree by the Commission hearings. However, only 94 of the 552 witnesses testified at the Commission hearings (the other witnesses either were questioned by the staff lawyers in the course of their field investigations or submitted affidavits).[1] In all, the Commission held forty-nine days of hearings, beginning on February 3, 1964, and ending on September 6, 1964—an average of about seven hearings per month.[2]

Commission hearings were defined by the presence of "one or more members of the Commission." With one exception, the hearings were closed to the public.[3] The witnesses had the right to be advised by counsel, but few availed themselves of this right. Most of the hearings were held in the Commission's offices in Washington, although on two occasions they were held in Texas.[4] Most of the basic evidence was introduced into the record at such hearings.

Although these hearings served to substantiate and formalize the findings of the investigation, they produced little, if any, new evidence of consequence. As Commissioner Ford wrote, "There were no startling developments, no sudden turns of evidence that opened up truths previously unperceived."[5] Possibly no new evidence or "truths" came to light because all the significant facts were already known. There were, however, other possible reasons why the Commission hearings did not uncover new evidence on the assassination.

First of all, only a minor portion of the hearings was devoted to testimony relating to the assassination itself. By far the greatest portion of the Commission's time was occupied with testimony concerning Lee Harvey Oswald's biography. The hearings began and ended with the testimony of Marina Oswald, and it accounted for more than 12 per cent of the total Commission hearings. Although Marina Oswald might possibly have cast light on Oswald's prior movements and motives, she seemed to have no direct knowledge of the assassination itself.

The testimony of Oswald's mother and brother, neither of whom had seen Oswald for more than a year prior to the assassination, accounted for another 14 per cent of the hearings. Another 13 per cent was spent on the testimony of the people with whom the Lee Harvey Oswalds had resided at one time or another. In all, 43 per cent of the Commission's time was spent hearing testimony concerning Oswald's life history —a fact which suggests that the main focus of the Commission hearings was Oswald, not the assassination itself.

The Commission also spent considerable time—about 12 per cent of the hearings—on testimony concerning the operation of government agencies. The Commission dealt with such questions as: How was Oswald able to return to the United

States after defecting to the Soviet Union? Why was Oswald not under closer FBI surveillance? Were the Secret Service's protective measures adequate?

A number of prominent witnesses, such as Secretary of State Dean Rusk, Secretary of the Treasury Douglas Dillon, FBI Director J. Edgar Hoover, and Director of Central Intelligence John McCone, testified on the procedures of their agencies.[6] Although the inclusion of these notable witnesses gave stature and importance to the Commission's investigation, it did not serve to reveal any new facts about the assassination itself.

The Commission also spent considerable time on other peripheral problems such as the methods of the Dallas police, the activities of Jack Ruby, and anti-Kennedy advertisements. The Commission was obliged to explore all these matters, because they might possibly have been connected with the assassination, but these explorations left little time for testimony concerning the assassination itself.

Thus, less than one-third of the Commission hearings— about 81 hours out of a total of 244—dealt with the pertinent facts of the assassination: the source of the shots, the identity of the assassin, and Oswald's movements on the day of the assassination. During these 81 hours of pertinent hearings, 51 witnesses testified. Most of the evidence was presented by expert witnesses, whose testimony concerned such complex subjects as forensic pathology, ballistics, fingerprints, hair and fiber analysis, etc. Quite obviously the Commission had neither the time nor technical knowledge to scrutinize the expert testimony. Although expert testimony also presents a problem in judicial trials, the problem is usually solved by adversary proceedings in which the defense counsel calls expert witnesses to challenge those of the prosecution.

One Commission lawyer, Melvin Eisenberg, did call "outside" expert witnesses to confirm the government expert wit-

nesses, but this was only done in the case of fingerprint and
ballistic identification.[7] In other areas, however, expert testimony received only cursory examination. For example, the
autopsy surgeon indicated in his testimony that the first bullet
that struck Kennedy passed through his body without leaving
a discernible "track" or path.[8] This testimony, however, contradicts a basic precept of forensic pathology: a rifle bullet
traveling through the body will *always* leave a path.[9] An outside expert witness might very well have clarified this apparent discrepancy, but such a process of critical re-examination
would also have required considerably more time than the
Commission could allot even to pertinent evidence.

Thus, although the members of the Commission asked
many perceptive questions of the witnesses, the depth to
which the hearings could probe was limited to some degree
by the relatively small amount of time the Commission devoted to hearing evidence on the assassination itself.

A second possible reason why the hearings failed to uncover new information was that virtually all the witnesses had
made statements to the federal investigators or to the staff
lawyers *before* they testified at the Commission hearings; the
only exceptions were the federal agents themselves and Mrs.
John F. Kennedy. Thus, at the hearings, not only would witnesses tend to adhere to their prior statements but quite probably they would remember their written statements more
clearly than the event itself.

For instance, four months after the assassination, Harold
Norman, a witness who was on the fifth floor of the Texas
Book Depository at the time of the assassination, testified in
great detail as to how he head heard the bolt of a rifle clicking
and rifle cartridges falling on the floor with every shot fired.[10]
Commissioner Ford said that he considered Norman's testimony important in pinpointing the source of the shots, and
that he was especially impressed with Norman's "remarkable

clarity and spontaneity."[11] However, less than a week before Norman testified at the Commission hearings he and many of the other eyewitnesses took part in a re-enactment. A Secret Service agent stood on the floor above Norman and worked the bolt of the rifle (without firing it) and dropped cartridges on the floor.[12] Therefore it was quite possible that Norman's "remarkable clarity" and "spontaneity" came from his memory of the re-enactment rather than the assassination. In any case, very few witnesses contradicted their written statements and gave new evidence.

When a witness did give new evidence in the Commission hearings, it became suspect *ipso facto*, because it was not included in a prior statement. For example, Arnold Rowland testified before the Commission that he had seen a second man on the same floor with the assassin. The Commission, however, rejected this portion of Rowland's testimony partly because of "Rowland's failure to report his story despite several interviews until his appearance before the Commission."[13] It will be recalled that Rowland insisted that he *did* mention this fact to FBI agents but that they were interested only in whether or not he could positively identify the assassin.[14] The Commission never called the FBI agents as witnesses on this matter.

By judging the testimony of witnesses by the standard of their prior statements, the Commission virtually precluded the possibility that new evidence would arise to alter significantly the basic suppositions concerning the assassination.

Some of the staff lawyers thought the Commission hearings were "a joke."[15] Liebeler said that most of the Commissioners were absent most of the time, and that they would stop in "for a few minutes," ask a question "which blew the lawyer's entire line of questioning," and then "rushed out to make a quorum or something."[16] Ball said that he spent considerable time "talking to an empty room."[17]

Although the staff no doubt tended to exaggerate the Commissioners' absenteeism, the attendance records of the Commission show that most of the Commissioners were present for only a minor portion of the hearings. Senator Russell, who attended the fewest, heard only about 6 per cent of the testimony; whereas Allen Dulles, who attended the largest number of hearings, heard about 71 per cent. Only three Commissioners heard more than half the testimony, and the average Commissioner heard 45 per cent.

J. Lee Rankin, however, asserted that the Commission members were "extremely dedicated" and that they would attend whenever they could leave their other responsibilities. For example, Rankin noted that even though Warren had to attend the Supreme Court every day it was in session, he arranged for Commission hearings to commence at 9 a.m. so that he could officially open them before he left for the Court at 10 a.m. Rankin said, "I worried about Warren's health because he was trying to do two full-time jobs at once."[18] Yet, regardless of efforts and good intentions, the fact remained that the Commissioners had other responsibilities and they could spend only part of their time at Commission hearings.[19]

Rankin also pointed out that some of the lawyers were so engrossed in their own investigations that they were not always aware of the work of the Commission.[20] Most lawyers agreed that the separation between the staff investigation and the Commission hearings tended to widen as the investigation progressed.

The degree of separation between staff and Commission is illustrated by an incident involving Commissioner McCloy. McCloy said that he found that the administrative assistant, Howard Willens, "had locked information away in his top drawer" and at first refused him access to the material.[21] McCloy then discussed the matter with Warren, and, according to McCloy, Warren ordered Willens to make all the material available to the individual Commissioners.[22] Rankin explained that this incident was caused by an "unfortunate misunderstanding," and that Willens was withholding the information because he was waiting for other corroborative evidence.[23] In any case, this incident shows that the Commission was somewhat detached from the work of the staff.

Rankin further said that some of the younger lawyers simply didn't understand how a government investigation functions. He explained that it was important "for the sake of public, as well as historic, acceptance of the Report that the main evidence be brought directly before the Commission."[24] The function of the Commission hearings, then, was to record, rather than to investigate, the evidence.

7

The Hypothesis

On December 9, 1963, shortly after the first Commission meeting, the FBI submitted the Summary Report of its investigation to the Commission.[1] This report contained the seven major facts upon which the Commission, nine months later, explicitly predicated its main conclusion—that Oswald had assassinated President Kennedy.[2] If all the major facts were already established, what were the contributions of the independent investigation?

Norman Redlich said that, although the FBI established the basic facts, the independent investigation determined the relationships between these facts.[3] According to Redlich, the single most important contribution of the investigation was the theory that explained how one man, acting alone, committed the assassination.[4] The way in which this theory developed reveals to some extent the basic orientation of the investigation.

The FBI Version

The December 9, 1963, FBI Summary Report gives the following description of the assassination:

> As the motorcade was traveling through downtown Dallas on Elm Street about fifty yards west of the intersection with Houston Street . . . , three shots rang out. Two bullets struck President Kennedy, and one wounded Governor Connally.[5]

Although this account appeared to be basically accurate, the Commission's staff felt that for "the sake of the historical record" the sequence of events should be ascertained with greater precision.[6] Thus, through an analysis of the Zapruder film of the assassination and other relevant evidence, the staff attempted to determine the exact position of the car at the time of each shot and the time interval between the shots.[7]

The Film Analysis

On January 27, 1964, Norman Redlich, Melvin Eisenberg, and Arlen Specter of the Commission staff met with FBI photographic expert Lyndal Shaneyfelt, Secret Service Inspector Thomas Kelley, and FBI visual-aids expert Leo Gauthier to conduct a frame-by-frame analysis of the film.[8] The first problem was determining the exact position of the Presidential limousine at the time of the first shot.[9]

The latest point at which the President could have been

first hit is film frame 225. On this film frame it is evident that the President has been wounded.[10] The earliest point at which the President could have been hit was fixed by an oak tree. The Secret Service re-enactment of the assassination showed that the assassin's line of sight was blocked by the foliage of the large oak tree between film frame 166 and film frame 207.[11] The film further shows that the President is smiling and waving on film frame 207, and this makes it highly improbable that the President was shot before film frame 166. Moreover, still photographs and virtually all the eyewitnesses place the car past the oak tree at the time of the first shot. It was thus concluded that the first shot could have been fired only after film frame 207. The staff was able through this analysis of the film to fix the position of the car, at the time of the first shot, within eighteen film frames (about sixteen feet).

However, establishing the position of the car at the time of the first shot raised a new and more serious problem. The FBI had established that the murder weapon could not be fired twice in less than 2.3 seconds. This minimum time was based on the time it took to open and close the bolt of the rifle.[12] In terms of the film, 2.3 seconds are equivalent to 42 film frames—at the camera's established speed of 18.3 frames per second. This meant that the shots had to be spaced at least 42 frames apart on the film to be consistent with the minimum firing time of the assassination weapon. Since the first shot could not have been fired before film frame 207, a second shot from the same rifle could not have been fired before film frame 249. Thus it was initially assumed that Connally was hit after film frame 249, even though this was not apparent in the film.[13]

On February 25, 1964, the Commission finally obtained the original copy of the Zapruder film from *Life* magazine. Up to this point the staff had been using a second-generation copy (i.e., a copy of a copy).[14] The original film is considerably more detailed, and it shows that Governor Connally was hit well before film frame 249.[15] Subsequently Connally's doctors testified that Connally was not in a position to have been hit after film frame 240.[16]

Thus there are only 33 frames on the film between the earliest time at which Kennedy could first have been shot and the latest time at which Connally could have been shot. Yet the murder weapon could not be fired twice within this time period. A new working hypothesis thus would have to be found to explain the assassination.

The Single-Bullet Hypothesis

In early March, Arlen Specter discussed the time problem informally with Commanders James J. Humes and J. Thornton Boswell, the United States Navy doctors who had performed the autopsy on President Kennedy. According to Specter, Commander Humes suggested that since both Kennedy and Connally apparently had been hit within a second of each other, it was medically possible that both men had been hit by the same bullet and that Connally had had a delayed reaction.[17] This hypothesis would explain how both men were wounded in less time than that in which the murder weapon could be fired twice, but it raised another problem.

If both men were hit by the first bullet, quite obviously the first bullet must have exited from the front of the President's body. However, it will be recalled that the FBI Summary Report states that the autopsy revealed that the bullet in question did *not* exit from the front of the President's body.[18]

On March 16, 1964, the Commission heard testimony concerning the autopsy. On this day an undated autopsy report was introduced in evidence. Commander Humes testified that this autopsy report was prepared immediatedly after the autopsy examination and submitted to "higher authority" on November 24, 1963.[19] He also submitted an affidavit to the Commission, purportedly written on November 24, 1963, stating that he "destroyed by burning certain preliminary notes relating to" the autopsy.[20]

The autopsy report contains a conclusion that is diametrically opposed to the FBI's statement on the autopsy. The autopsy report states that the first bullet hit the President in the rear of the neck and *exited* from his throat, whereas the FBI Summary and Supplemental Reports stated that the autopsy found that the bullet in question hit the President below the shoulder and "penetrated to a distance of less than a finger length."[21]

If the FBI's statements are accurate, it would appear that the autopsy findings were revised some time subsequent to January 13, 1964.

Commander Humes testified that, although no bullet path was found through the President's body, it was deductively concluded that the bullet did indeed pass through the body and exit at the throat.[22] Commander Boswell, who assisted Commander Humes in the autopsy examination, testified that the autopsy report's conclusions were based on the autopsy and the "subsequent conference."[23]

When Commander Humes was asked what had happened to the bullet that had exited from the President's throat, Specter interjected: "That is the subject of some theories I am about to get into. That is an elusive subject, but Doctor Humes has some views on it."[24]

Thereupon Humes explained:

I see that Governor Connally is sitting directly in front of the late President, and suggest the possibility that this missile, having traversed the low neck of the late President, in fact traversed the chest of Governor Connally.[25]

The single-bullet hypothesis was thus advanced to the Commission.

Melvin Eisenberg said that "at first, some lawyers were incredulous of this hypothesis"[26]; but gradually they became persuaded that this was the only reasonable way to explain the fact that both men had been hit within a second or two of each other. Although the single-bullet hypothesis solved the time problem, it raised new problems.

First of all, there was the problem of the nearly whole bullet (bullet 399) found on a stretcher in the Dallas hospital where President Kennedy and Governor Connally were first treated. It was "preliminarily" thought, according to Specter, that this bullet had come from Kennedy's stretcher.[27]

However, *if* both men were both first hit by the same bullet, this nearly whole bullet could *not* have come from Kennedy's stretcher. According to the single-bullet hypothesis, the first bullet went through the President and Connally, the second bullet missed the car completely, and the third bullet hit the President's head and fragmented. Thus, the single-bullet hypothesis could be maintained only if the nearly whole bullet came from Connally's stretcher.

On March 16, the day when the single-bullet hypothesis was first advanced to the Commission, Specter told Dulles that there was evidence which showed that the bullet was found on Connally's, not Kennedy's, stretcher.[28] However, it will be recalled, there was *no* evidence at this time that indicated the bullet came from Connally's stretcher.[29] Subsequently evidence developed which all but precluded the possibility that the bullet had come from Connally's stretcher. Colonel Finck, a qualified expert in both forensic medicine and wound ballistics, testified that the bullet found on the stretcher could not be the bullet that caused Connally's wrist wound, primarily because more fragments were found in the wrist than were missing from the bullet.[30] The other medical witnesses agreed with this conclusion.[31] Yet, since other expert testimony and evidence precluded the possibility that Connally's wrist wound was caused by a fragment from the third bullet, or by a direct hit from another bullet, the Commission concluded that all Connally's wounds were caused by a single bullet.[32] The bullet found on the stretcher thus could not have been the bullet that caused all Connally's wounds. Nevertheless, despite this inconsistency, it was maintained that the bullet came from Connally's stretcher.

A second problem involved the testimony of Governor Connally in April. Connally testified that it was inconceivable to him that he was hit by the first shot because he distinctly remembered hearing the first shot before he had felt the impact of the bullet striking.[33] Since a bullet travels faster than the speed of sound, Connally reasoned that he could have been hit only by the second bullet.[34] The evidence clearly indicated that Kennedy had been hit by the first bullet.[35]

Connally's contention that he was hit by a separate shot was corroborated by his wife, who testified that *after* the first shot she saw "the President as he had both hands at his neck," and a few seconds later "there was the second shot that hit John [Connally]."[36] Of the more than one hundred eyewitnesses to the assassination, not one testified that both men were hit by the same shot.

It is possible, although unlikely,[37] that Connally did not immediately perceive his wound, or that his memory of the event was confused. However, there was other evidence which corroborated Connally's account.

Both of Connally's doctors testified, on the basis of their

medical knowledge of the case as well as of a careful study of the film of the assassination, that Connally was hit *after* film frame 231.[38] Yet, it will be recalled, the film showed that the President was definitely hit by frame 225. Thus, according to the medical testimony, there was an absolute minimum of six film frames between the time Kennedy and Connally were hit. This leads one to the conclusion that the two men were hit by two bullets.

In order to maintain the single-bullet hypothesis it was necessary to assume that other evidence was erroneous. First, it had to be assumed that the FBI Summary and Supplemental Reports' statements on the autopsy were inaccurate. Second, it had to be assumed that expert testimony which precluded the possibility that the bullet found on the stretcher was the bullet that wounded Connally was incorrect. Third, it had to be assumed Connally himself was wrong in his impression that he was hit by a separate bullet. Finally, it had to be assumed that Connally's doctors were mistaken in their conclusion that Connally was not in a position to be hit before film frame 231. The fact that this hypothesis was maintained and further tested indicates to some degree the investigation's commitment to an explanation of the assassination based on a "lone assassin" premise.

The Tests

On April 27, 1964, United States Army wound ballistics experts conducted further tests on the murder weapon. Arlen Specter, who supervised these tests, said that their primary purpose was to determine the penetrating power of the bullets, and specifically whether or not the bullets would penetrate a second object after exiting from the initial object.[39] In other words, the wound ballistics tests were meant to "test" the single-bullet hypothesis.

Colonel Finck testified that properly to test the single-bullet hypothesis it would be necessary to pass a bullet through two human cadavers.[40] However, Specter said that it was "too complicated" to fire a bullet through two objects at a time; thus, in the wound ballistics tests, bullets were not fired through more than one object at a time.[41] Three series of tests were held. In the first series, bullets were fired from the murder weapon through an object (gelatin blocks) which simulated the President's neck. By measuring the average entrance and exit speed of the bullets, it was determined that the bullets lost about 82 feet per second from an original velocity of about 2000 feet per second, traveling through the gelatin. In the second series of tests, bullets were fired from the murder weapon through an anesthetized goat, which simulated Governor Connally's chest, and it was determined that the bullets lost about 265 feet per second. In the third series of tests, bullets were fired through the wrist of a cadaver, which simulated Connally's wrist, and it was determined that a direct hit caused far more damage to the wrist than Connally actually had suffered.[42]

Doctor Alfred Olivier, the veterinarian who conducted the wound ballistics tests, testified before the Commission in May on the results of the test. When asked if the tests had indicated that Connally and Kennedy were hit by the same bullet, he replied: "My feeling is that it would be more probable that it [the bullet which struck the wrist] passed through the President first."[43]

Doctor Olivier explained that this conclusion was based on the fact that a direct hit caused considerably more damage to the simulated wrist than Connally's wrist actually had suffered. Therefore it was deduced that the bullet which had hit

Connally's wrist had passed through a prior object. In the tests, the bullet had lost 265 feet per second when it passed through the goat that simulated Connally's chest. Because Connally's chest is about half again as wide as the goat, it was assumed that the bullet would have lost 400 feet per second passing through Connally's chest.[44] Doctor Olivier estimated that the bullet that struck the wrist had lost at least 480 feet per second, and therefore he concluded that the bullet must have passed through a third object—the President's neck.[45]

This conclusion was based on the assumption that the conditions of the experiment closely simulated those of the assassination. However, this was not in fact the case. Since the conclusion that Kennedy and Connally were hit by the same bullet is based on a difference of only about 80 feet per second in the bullet's velocity (4 per cent of the bullet's initial velocity), the disparity between the width of Connally and the goat might be a significant one. The attempt to compensate for the disparity simply by adding 50 per cent to the loss of velocity is at best a dubious extrapolation. The deceleration function for a bullet passing through a non-uniform substance, such as a goat, no doubt requires a more complicated computation. In any case, the fact remains that the goat did not even approximately simulate Connally's chest.

Further doubt was cast on the results of the wound ballistics tests by the testimony of Doctor Frederick E. Light, the medical pathologist associated with the tests. Dr. Light was asked whether he agreed with Dr. Olivier's conclusion that both the President and Governor Connally were hit by the same bullet. He replied:

> I am not quite as sure in my mind as I believe he [Olivier] is that the bullet that struck the Governor was almost certainly one which had hit something else first. I believe

it could have produced that [wrist] wound even though it hadn't hit the President or any other person or object first.[46]

Specter then asked Dr. Light if the same amount of damage would have been inflicted on Connally's wrist if the bullet had *not* passed through the President first. Dr. Light answered:

I think that is possible; yes. It won't happen the same way twice in any case, so you have got a fairly wide range of things that can happen if a person is shot in more or less this way.[47]

The wound ballistics tests were thus inconclusive as to whether or not the President and Governor Connally were hit by the same bullet.

The Reconstruction

In May, Specter proposed that the Commission conduct a reconstruction of the assassination based on the film in order to determine whether Connally and Kennedy were hit by the same bullet.[48] Specter said that the Commissioners initially opposed a reconstruction, "because they felt it would look bad at this late date to show that the basic facts were not known."[49] Rankin, however, gave a different reason; he said that the Commission was reluctant to permit a reconstruction for fear that "an overenthusiastic lawyer" might "make the facts fit the hypothesis." Thus the Commission agreed to the reconstruction only on the condition that it would be supervised personally by Rankin.[50]

On May 23, 1964, Rankin, Redlich, and Specter went to

Dallas to conduct the reconstruction. The next morning the sequence of events of the assassination was meticulously reconstructed. An open limousine, with stand-ins for Kennedy and Connally, simulated the movements of the Presidential limousine on the day of the assassination. The limousine was slowly pushed until its position coincided exactly with the position of the limousine shown in the film of the assassination; at each point a photograph was taken from the "sniper's nest" in the Texas Book Depository through the telescopic sight of the murder rifle. In this manner, each film frame was correlated with the assassin's line of sight, and the trajectory was measured. Through this reconstruction it was possible to determine the assassin's view and the trajectory on each of the three shots.[51]

On June 4, 1964, the federal agents who participated in this reconstruction testified before the Commission. FBI ballistics expert Robert Frazier, who had occupied the position of the assassin during the test, was asked if it was probable that the bullet "which passed through the neck of the President" hit Governor Connally.[52] Frazier replied:

> There are a lot of probables in that. First, we have to assume that there is absolutely no deflection in the bullet from the time it left the barrel until the time it exited from the Governor's body.[53]

Frazier said that it was "entirely possible" that both men were hit by the same bullet, but he continued:

> I myself don't have any technical evidence which would permit me to say one way or the other, in other words which would support it as far as my rendering an opinion as an expert. I would certainly say it was possible but I don't say that it probably occurred because I don't have the evidence on which to base a statement like that.[54]

Specter then asked what evidence was missing, and Frazier answered:

We are dealing with hypothetical situations here in placing people in cars from photographs which are not absolutely accurate. They are two dimensional. They don't give you the third dimension.

Secondly, we are dealing with the fact that we don't know whether, I don't know technically, whether there was any deviation in the bullet which struck the President in the back and exited from his front. If there was a few degrees deviation then it may affect my opinion as to whether or not it would have struck the Governor.[55]

Frazier was then asked how the bullet could possibly have exited from the President, missed Connally, and also escaped hitting the car. He replied:

I have seen bullets strike small twigs, small objects, and ricochet for no apparent reason except they hit and all the pressure is on one side and it turns the bullet and it goes off at an angle.[56]

Frazier, the only expert witness to testify on the path of the bullet and the probability of its hitting both men, thus refused to support the single-bullet hypothesis.

Like the wound ballistics tests, the reconstruction showed only that it was *possible* that both men were hit by a single bullet; it did not show that it was *probable*.

Specter, however, considered both tests to be "very important corroborative evidence" that both men were hit by the same bullet.[57]

By June 5 Specter had submitted his chapter on the basic facts of the assassination.[58] The facts and premises set forth in the chapter were selected and organized so as to support the single-bullet hypothesis.[59] Even after the chapter was toned down by the Commission, it asserted:

> Frazier testified that it [the bullet which first hit Kennedy] probably struck Governor Connally.[60]

And on the basis of this statement the single-bullet hypothesis was advanced.

However, as has been previously shown, Frazier explicitly had refused to testify as to the probability of both men being hit by the same bullet, and he had clearly enumerated his reasons for not doing so.

Frazier thus did *not* testify that the bullet that hit the President "probably struck Governor Connally." This statement apparently referred to an answer that Frazier had made to a hypothetical question.[61] When asked by Commissioner Ford to *assume* (1) that the bullet had passed through Kennedy and continued in an absolutely straight line, and (2) that Governor Connally was seated directly in the path of that bullet; Frazier had replied that "under those conditions," the bullet "had to" have hit Connally.[62] However, he qualified this answer by stating that he had no "technical evidence" on which to base these assumptions.[63]

The statement of probability attributed to Frazier was thus inaccurate and misleading.

In addition, the chapter cited the wound ballistics tests as "further" evidence that both men were hit by the same bullet, explaining:

> Correlation of a test simulating the Governor's chest wound with the neck and wrist experiment indicated that course.[64]

This correlation, as has been shown, was predicated on a very dubious assumption. In any case, the wound ballistics tests were admittedly inconclusive.

The single-bullet hypothesis was thus advanced on the basis of a misinterpretation of Frazier's ballistics testimony, and substantiated by the extremely tenuous findings of the wound ballistics tests. Evidence that was inconsistent with the single-bullet hypothesis, such as Colonel Finck's testimony concerning the bullet found on a stretcher, was omitted from the chapter. The hypothesis thus tended, in a sense, to be a self-fulfilling prophecy.

Norman Redlich said that he considered the single-bullet theory one of the most important contributions of the independent investigation.[65] Indeed, this theory involved the only substantial change from the basic facts that were established in the FBI Summary and Supplemental Reports. Despite the fact that the staff felt that this theory was the only reasonable way to explain the sequence of events in terms of a single assassin, and no alternate hypotheses were considered, in the final analysis the Commission—for reasons to be discussed later—refused to accept the single-bullet theory.[66]

PART THREE

The Report

8

Writing the Report

THE COMMISSION had two distinct tasks: the investigation and the writing of the Report. J. Lee Rankin said, "No one realized how long it would take to write the Report; instead of the estimated one month, it took nearly four months to complete."[1] The original plan was for each team of lawyers to write a chapter about its own investigative area and for all teams to submit their chapters to the Commission by June 1.[2]

However, most of the lawyers had not even completed their field investigations by June. Therefore, to expedite the writing of the Report, Rankin appointed Norman Redlich, Alfred Goldberg, Howard Willens, and himself as a "Re-editing Committee." Redlich was assigned editorial responsibility for the first four chapters in the Report; Goldberg, for the next three chapters; and Willens, for the eighth and final chapter.[3]

Rankin acted as intermediary between the Commission and the staff in the writing of the Report.[4]

The first four chapters concerned the assassination itself. Chapter I was a brief seventeen-page summary of the event, which Redlich wrote himself.[5]

The second chapter was a more detailed narrative of the assassination, which began with the advance planning for the Dallas trip and ended with the return of the President's body to Washington. Although Arlen Specter and Samuel Stern made some contributions to the writing of this chapter, it was written mainly by Redlich.[6]

The third chapter focused on the basic facts of the assassination: the source of the shots, the sequence of events, medical findings, etc. This chapter was originally written by Specter and submitted by the June deadline. However, a basic premise of the chapter was that the President and Governor Connally were hit by the same bullet. When the Commission refused to accept this premise, the chapter had to be substantially rewritten by Redlich.[7]

The fourth chapter, which Redlich considered to be "the crucial chapter," dealt with the evidence that identified the assassin as Lee Harvey Oswald.[8] The original chapter was written by Joseph Ball and David Belin, who had investigated the evidence, but in late June the Re-editing Committee rejected this chapter as "totally inadequate."[9] Redlich then undertook to rewrite the chapter himself—a task which took over ten weeks and which involved the very difficult problem of selecting evidence, a problem which will be more fully discussed later.[10] Chapter IV, in effect, presented the case against Oswald.

The next three chapters, for which Goldberg had editorial responsibility, concerned peripheral events. Chapter V dealt with the circumstances of Oswald's death and the actions of Jack Ruby. Because the lawyers who were investigating the area, Burt Griffin and Leon Hubert, Jr., had continued their field investigation well into July, Rankin assigned Murray Laulicht, a twenty-four-year-old law clerk, to assist in writing the chapter.[11] In August the chapter was finally written by Griffin and Laulicht, but Goldberg found the style cumbersome, and he completely rewrote the chapter himself.[12]

The sixth chapter concerned possible conspiracies involving Oswald. Stuart Pollak, a Department of Justice lawyer who participated in the investigation, wrote the part of the chapter on Oswald's movements abroad; and W. David Slawson wrote the balance of the chapter. Pollak then rewrote the entire chapter. Goldberg, however, found that the chapter did not satisfactorily deal with the problem of alleged conspiracies, and he therefore rewrote most of the chapter and supplemented it with an appendix dealing with specific "speculations and rumors."[13]

Chapter VII, about Oswald's background and possible motives, was originally written by Wesley Liebeler, the lawyer who investigated this area. Although it was considered the "most brilliant chapter," the Commission found it "too subtle" and "too sympathetic."[14] Goldberg therefore revised the chapter and rewrote portions of it.[15]

The final chapter was on the general problem of Presidential protection. Samuel Stern wrote the draft chapter, but the Commission considered the treatment of the Secret Service "not critical enough," and Howard Willens rewrote a substantial part of the chapter.[16]

Rankin said that he did not send "the first few drafts" of the chapters to the Commission, because they were "too rough."[17] After the Re-editing Committee had "worked out" initial problems in the chapters, they were sent to the individual Commissioners for comments.[18] The Commissioners toned down the adjectives used in the chapters, raised questions about certain points, and wrote comments in the margins.[19]

The Commissioners' criticisms and comments were then collated by the Re-editing Committee, and portions of the chapters were returned to the lawyers to be rewritten. Some chapters were rewritten as many as twenty times before all the Commissioners were satisfied. Through this process, the Commissioners' comments and judgments were incorporated into the Report.[20]

Finally, the evidence relied on in the Report had to be cited in the twenty-six volumes of testimony and exhibits.[21] Approximately twenty young lawyers assisted the staff in the process of cite-checking. If a statement in the Report was not fully supported by the evidence, then, at least theoretically, it had to be modified or deleted.[22] By September, however, most of the lawyers were extremely reluctant to make changes in their chapters. One lawyer, concerned about this attitude, wrote:

> Eight months' work of the Commission and staff is in serious danger of being nullified because of the present impatience to publish. . . . Staff members are becoming increasingly unwilling to discuss change or refinement, which would cause a printing delay.[23]

Time pressure thus affected the writing of the Report as it had affected the investigation.

The final draft of the Report was completed in mid-September. Rankin then assigned Goldberg the task of "polishing it up."[24] Goldberg said that he needed six months to do a competent rewriting job, and he had less than one week.[25]

The Warren Report—a 469-page document, supplemented by eighteen appendices[26]—was finally made public on September 28, 1964. Who wrote the Report? Although more than thirty persons had had a hand in writing it, it was written mainly by two men: Norman Redlich and Alfred Goldberg.

9

The Selection Process

Americans often assume that facts are solid, concrete (and discrete) objects like marbles, but they are very much not. Rather are they subtle essences, full of mystery and metaphysics, that change their color and shape, their meaning, according to the context in which they are presented. They must always be treated with skepticism and the standard of judgment should be not how many facts one can mobilize in support of a position but how skillfully one discriminates between them, how objectively one uses them to arrive at Truth, which is something different from, though not unrelated to, the Facts.
— DWIGHT MACDONALD[1]

THE MAJOR PROBLEM in the writing of the Report was the selection of evidence. From the tens of thousands of pages of evidence, which facts were to be included, and which facts excluded?

In a trial this problem of selecting evidence is pragmatically solved through the adversary system. The prosecutor and the defense counsel each select those facts which support his own case. The two opposing sets of facts are then reduced, through the dialectical process, to provide a basis for judgment.

However, the writers of the Report quite obviously could not simply select the evidence that supported their case, or the Report would have been of no more value than a prosecutor's brief which was not tested or challenged by a defense counsel. Norman Redlich thought the problem could be solved by the "impartial selection of facts,"[2] but Liebeler skeptically told him, "I suggest, Norman, that you start to make an argument the minute you select a fact."[3]

The difficulties encountered in attempting to select evidence impartially can best be seen in Chapter IV, which sets forth the case against Oswald. The way in which the facts were selected for this chapter reveals, to some extent, the criteria and objectives which governed the writing of the Report.

As had been noted, Chapter IV was first written by Joseph Ball and David Belin, the lawyers who investigated the evidence in this area. However, when the Re-editing Committee found the chapter "totally inadequate," Norman Redlich undertook to rewrite it.[4]

Joseph Ball said that the main difference between his version of the chapter and Redlich's was the "style of writing."[5] Ball claimed to have used "a concise, narrative style"; whereas, Redlich, according to Ball, preferred "a turgid, 'Law Review' style."[6] There were, however, other, more substantial differences between the two chapters.

The Three New Witnesses

Ball said that his chapter relied more on "hard, scientific evidence" and less on eyewitness evidence than did Redlich's.[7] For example, Ball had rejected as "utterly unreliable" the testimony of Helen Louise Markham, who was the only witness who claimed to have seen Oswald shoot Dallas policeman J. D. Tippit.[8] Ball found Mrs. Markham's testimony to be "full of mistakes." For example, although Mrs. Markham claimed that Oswald leaned into Tippit's police car, photographs taken immediately after the shooting showed that the car window was closed. Also, although Mrs. Markham claimed to have spoken to Tippit while waiting for the ambulance, medical evidence showed that he died instantaneously. Finally, although Mrs. Markham claimed she was the only witness at the scene, there were a number of witnesses present.[9] Ball characterized Mrs. Markham as an unconvincing witness, and he said that, in view of other available evidence, her testimony was not needed for the case against Oswald.[10]

However, when the chapter was rewritten, Mrs. Markham's testimony was given considerable weight, and the description of Tippit's murder was based mainly on her account of the event.[11] Wesley Liebeler, the lawyer who had examined Mrs. Markham, told Redlich that the woman's testimony was "contradictory" and "worthless."[12] However, Redlich had replied, "The Commission wants to believe Mrs. Markham and that's all there is to it."[13] In a subsequent memorandum Liebeler warned that accepting Mrs. Markham's testimony "played into [Mark] Lane's hands" and left the Report open to criticism.[14] At last, after a heated exchange with Liebeler, Redlich agreed to qualify Mrs. Markham's testimony, and it was assigned only "probative" value.[15]

Ball was also extremely dubious of the testimony of Howard L. Brennan, the only eyewitness who claimed he could identify the assassin as Oswald.[16] At the time of the assassination Brennan was across the street from the Texas Book Depository, about 120 feet from the sixth-floor window from which the shots came. Later that day Brennan said at a police lineup that he could not identify Oswald as the assassin.[17] In January, when asked by the FBI, Brennan still insisted that he could not identify Oswald as the assassin.[18] However, when Brennan appeared before the Commission in March he said that he *could* identify the assassin as Oswald, and that he had lied at the police lineup to protect himself and his family.[19]

Ball had several reasons to doubt Brennan's testimony. First of all, in staging a "reconstruction" of the assassination on March 20, 1964, Ball found that Brennan had difficulty seeing a figure in the window, and thus it seemed doubtful that Brennan could have positively identified a man in the partially opened sixth-floor window 120 feet away.[20] Second, Brennan's identification was not based on prominent points in the assassin's clothes or dimensions. Third, Brennan's testimony contained a major error. Brennan stated that the assassin was standing while firing the rifle; other evidence, however, conclusively showed that the assassin fired from a kneeling or sitting position.[21] Finally, as far as Ball was concerned, the fact that Brennan had lied at the police lineup reflected on his general credibility.[22]

In rewriting the chapter, Redlich gave a great deal more weight to Brennan's identification than did Ball.[23] The section was subtitled "Eyewitness Identification of the Assassin," even though the Commission had never fully accepted Brennan's identification.[24] Redlich also added that "Brennan was in an excellent position to observe anyone in the window" and that "the record indicates Brennan was an accurate observer"— even though Brennan was *in*accurate in his description of the assassin's clothing and position.[25]

Although Ball found Marina Oswald to be "at best, an unreliable witness," Redlich based part of his version of the chapter on her testimony.[26] Redlich included, as one of the seven major points in the case against Oswald, Oswald's purported attempt to assassinate General Walker—despite the fact that Marina Oswald's testimony was the main evidence for this allegation and despite the fact that Mrs. Oswald had apparently fabricated or imagined Oswald's attempt to assassinate Richard Nixon.[27] Norman Redlich himself had asserted in February: ". . . Marina Oswald has lied to the Secret Service, the FBI, and this Commission on matters of vital concern. . . ."[28] Yet in rewriting the chapter Redlich chose to rely on Marina Oswald's testimony.[29]

Ball said that Helen Louise Markham, Howard Brennan, and Marina Oswald were not only unreliable witnesses but also unnecessary witnesses.[30] Yet Redlich gave added weight to the testimony of these witnesses.

It took nearly three months to rewrite Chapter IV. As Redlich said, "For a while, the job seemed endless."[31] Every fact had to be supported by other facts, every possibility had to be taken into account, every permutation had to be explored. And then, Redlich continued, there was the problem of consensus; every paragraph had to be written so that all seven Commissioners approved of it.[32]

Finally, on September 4, 1964, Chapter IV was completed and sent to the printer.[33]

The Liebeler Memorandum

Wesley Liebeler read the galley proofs of Chapter IV on the weekend of September 5, and he was disconcerted by the quality of the writing. He later said, "It read like a brief for the prosecution."[34]

Over the weekend Liebeler wrote a 26-page single-spaced memorandum which attacked the chapter point by point and warned:

To put it bluntly, this sort of selection from the record

could seriously affect the integrity and credibility of the entire report.[35]

The memorandum, by its detailed analysis of the way facts were selected, provides an insight into the writing of the Report.

First of all, there was the problem of gaps in the case against Oswald. How were these gaps filled? For example, to eliminate the possibility that Oswald's rifle was used by another person, the Report had to show that the rifle was in Oswald's possession on the day of the assassination. The chapter therefore asserted that "evidence showed" that the rifle was in the Paines' home (where Marina Oswald temporarily resided) on the eve of the assassination, that Oswald visited his wife at the Paines' home that evening, that he left on the morning of the assassination with a "long, bulky package," and that after the assassination the rifle was missing from the Paines' home.[36] Yet, although all these "facts" appeared to provide cogent evidence that Oswald took the rifle on the day of the assassination, Liebeler pointed out an important gap in the chain of "evidence": there was no actual evidence that the rifle was in the Paines' home on the eve of the assassination.[37]

Marina Oswald had testified that the rifle was transported from New Orleans to Dallas in a blanket and that the blanket was stored in the Paines' garage.[38] In September, she said, she had looked inside the blanket and had seen part of a rifle, but in the seven weeks preceding the assassination she had not looked inside the blanket or handled it, and thus she had no way of knowing whether the blanket still contained the rifle. This fact was demonstrated immediately after the assassination, when Marina Oswald looked at the blanket without opening it and assumed the rifle was still inside it, although, as was later revealed, the blanket was empty.[39] No other witness saw the rifle in the blanket. Thus there was no evidence whatsoever that showed that the rifle was in the Paines' home between late September and the assassination, and it was conceivable that the rifle was removed sometime during this seven-week period. Liebeler noted: "Gaps cannot be filled by ignoring them."[40]

Second, there was the problem involving relevant evidence that was not cited. The chapter based its conclusion that Oswald carried the rifle in the "long, bulky package" mainly on the testimony of two witnesses, Linnie Mae Randle, Oswald's neighbor, and Buell Wesley Frazier, who drove Oswald to work on the morning of the assassination. Both witnesses believed that the bag was less than 28 inches long. However, the wooden stock of the rifle was 34.8 inches long, and thus, if the witnesses' testimony was accurate, the bag could not have contained the rifle.[41] Mrs. Randle said that she had had only a glimpse of the bag, and therefore no weight was given to her estimate of length.[42] Frazier based his estimate of two feet "give and take a few inches" on the fact that Oswald held the package under his arm, cupping the bottom of it with his right hand.[43] The chapter stated: "Frazier could easily have been mistaken when he stated that Oswald held the bottom of the bag cupped in his hand with the upper end tucked under his arm pit."[44] There was, however, corroborative evidence for Frazier's description which was neglected at this point, although it was mentioned elsewhere in the chapter: Liebeler pointed out that the location of Oswald's right palm print on the bag—the heel and fingers were on the bottom of the bag exactly as if it had been "cupped"— indicated that Frazier's description *was* accurate.[45]

Third, Liebeler's memorandum noted in the chapter a tendency to "stretch" inconclusive scientific evidence by selecting testimony out of context and thus making it appear conclusive.[46] For example, the chapter stated that fibers found in the paper bag (found in the Depository) matched fibers in the blanket in which it was *assumed* that the rifle was stored; and that this fact further indicated that the bag was used to carry the rifle into the Depository.[47]

However, Liebeler indicated that the fiber evidence was extremely "thin."[48] Paul Stombaugh, the FBI expert who examined the fiber evidence, testified that since the two types of fibers found in the bag were most common types, and since the blanket contained thirty different types of fibers, of which only two matched the fibers found in the bag, there was insufficient evidence to judge whether or not it was probable that the fibers in the bag came from the blanket.[49] Stombaugh said, "All I would say here is that it is possible that these fibers could have come from this blanket."[50] Yet, even though Stombaugh refused to say it was probable that the fibers came from the blanket, the chapter asserted that the fiber evidence indicated that the bag had once contained the rifle.[51]

Another problem with the fiber evidence was omitted from the chapter: the fibers found on the rifle did not match either those found in the bag or those found in the blanket.[52] If the rifle had been stored in the blanket, as was assumed, one would expect some blanket fibers to have been found on the rifle, but none were. Quite obviously, fibers in the bag which matched fibers in the blanket had no value as evidence unless fibers were also found on the rifle—especially since there was no evidence that the rifle had been stored in the blanket immediately before the assassination. The fact that fibers on the rifle did not match fibers in the blanket possibly indicated that the blanket had not contained the rifle. Yet this portion of the fiber evidence was omitted from the Report.

Liebeler also criticized the way in which the chapter interpreted the fingerprint evidence. In reaching the conclusion that Oswald was at the window when the shots were fired, the chapter attached "great weight" to the fact that Oswald's fingerprints and palm prints were on the cardboard cartons found near the window from which the shots came.[53]

However, Liebeler pointed out that these were cartons that Oswald normally handled in the course of his work, and that the fingerprints thus showed only that Oswald had handled the cartons and not that he was at the window at the time of the assassination.[54]

The final part of the memorandum's analysis of the evidence dealt with Oswald's capabilities as a rifleman.

The first problem was to see whether Oswald could have fired three shots in 5.6 seconds. This time was determined from the film of the assassination. Because the assassin's view of the President was blocked by the oak tree until film frame 207, this was assumed to be earliest point at which the President could have been shot. On film frame 313, the last shot is clearly discernible. Using frame 210 as the earliest point, as the Report does, a maximum of 103 film frames elapsed between the first and last shot, and, since the camera speed was 18.3 frames per second, the maximum time that elapsed was 5.6 seconds. Thus it remained to be seen whether Oswald was capable of accurately firing the rifle three times in 5.6 seconds.[55]

The rifle tests held by the FBI and the Army were an important part of the evidence. The first tests with Oswald's rifle were conducted on November 27, 1963, by the FBI. Each of three rifle experts—Charles Killion, Cortlandt Cunningham, and Robert Frazier—fired three shots at a target fifteen yards away. All the shots were high and to the right of the aiming point: Killion's firing time was 9 seconds; Cunningham's firing time was 8 seconds; Frazier's firing time was 6 seconds.[56] Thus none of the FBI experts equaled Oswald's time, despite the fact that their target was stationary and only fifteen yards away; whereas Oswald's target was moving and more than sixty yards away.

Later the same day Frazier fired two more series of shots "to determine how fast the weapon could be fired primarily."[57] The first series of three shots was fired in 4.8 seconds, and the second one was fired in 4.6 seconds.[58] Frazier testified that firing in 4.6 seconds "is firing this weapon as fast as the bolt can be operated."[59]

The final FBI tests were held at Quantico, Virginia, on March 16, 1964. Frazier fired three series of shots at a target a hundred yards away. His time for the first series of three shots was 5.9 seconds; for the second series, 6.2 seconds; and for the third series, 6.5 seconds.[60] Not only did Frazier fail to equal Oswald's time of 5.6 seconds, but all his shots were about five inches high and about five inches to the right of the aiming point. Frazier explained in his testimony that the inaccuracy was due to an uncorrectable mechanical deficiency in the telescopic sights.[61]

The Commission evidently was not satisfied with the results of the FBI tests, because it arranged for the United States Army Ballistic Research Laboratory to conduct further tests on March 27, 1964.[62] Three rifle experts—Hendrix, Staley, and Miller, all of whom held Master rifle ratings from the National Rifle Association—fired at three silhouette targets located at distances matching the distances of the Presidential limousine from the source of the shots during the assassination.

Hendrix fired his first series of three bullets in 8.25 seconds and missed the second target; he fired his second series in 7.0 seconds and missed the third target. Staley fired his first series in 6.75 seconds and his second series in 6.45 seconds; both times he missed the second target. Miller was the only expert to equal Oswald's time; he fired his first series in 4.6 seconds and his second series in 5.5 seconds, although he missed the second target both times. Miller later fired a third series, using standard sights instead of telescopic sights. In this series he fired three shots in 4.45 seconds, but the third shot went wild and missed the board as well as the silhouette target.[63]

Although the Army tests demonstrated that it was at least possible to fire three shots in 5.6 seconds with the murder weapon, three factors must be taken into account in evaluating these tests.

First, the experts were timed only from the sound of the first shot to the sound of the last shot. This meant that they had *unlimited* time to aim at the first target and pull the trigger before they were timed.[64] The assassin, however, had only 5.6 seconds for all three shots from the moment the car first became visible, and thus his aiming time was included in the total time. This is a significant factor. For example, if it is assumed it took the assassin one second to react, aim, and pull the trigger, then he had only 4.6 seconds (*not* 5.6 seconds) to fire. Thus, in order to make comparisons, this aiming factor must be added to the experts' time.

Second, the experts were firing at a stationary target, whereas the assassin was firing at a moving target. FBI expert Robert Frazier, who supervised the FBI rifle tests, testified that a moving target "would have slowed down the shooting. It would have lengthened the time to the extent of allowing the crosshairs to pass over the moving target."[65] Frazier estimated this sighting time would be "approximately one second,"[66] but it is unclear whether he meant one second for each shot or for all three shots. In any case, this sighting time would also have to be added to the experts' time in order for comparisons to be made.

Finally, when the Army experts found that the sight could not be accurately aimed at a target, they added three "shims" to the sight to correct the inaccuracy.[67] Thus the Army experts fired with accurate sights, whereas, so far as is known, the assassin fired with inaccurate sights.

Despite the fact that only two of the six rifle experts were able to equal the assassin's time of 5.6 seconds, the draft chapter characterized the shots as "easy shots."[68] Statements were selected from four expert witnesses which appeared to support this characterization, but Liebeler pointed out that these selected statements pertained only to the distance and trajectory of the shots, and *not* to the time factor involved in firing.[69] In other words, the fact that the assassin had only 5.6 seconds to fire the three shots was not taken into account.

The manner in which this testimony was developed indicates that premeditation was involved in the selection process. The two witnesses who characterized the shots as "easy shots," Major Eugene Anderson and Sergeant James Zahm, were not called until July 24, 1964.[70] At this late date the investigation had been closed for more than a month, and Redlich was involved in rewriting the chapter. The date these witnesses testified thus suggests that they were called for the express purpose of characterizing the shots as "easy shots," and the type of questions they were asked seems to reflect this possibility.

Each witness was asked a hypothetical question in which the distance of the shot, the trajectory, and even the street downgrade were given, but the time factor was conspicuously omitted.[71] Therefore, in answering the question, neither witness had to take into account the most difficult problem, firing three shots in 5.6 seconds. Thus both witnesses characterized the shots as "not difficult" and "easy."[72]

Liebeler found these assertions to be contrary to the evidence, which showed that the shot was extremely difficult. The memorandum indicated that in 80 per cent of the tests in which accuracy was a primary concern the experts failed to equal Oswald's maximum time. Moreover, only one of the six experts accomplished this feat, and the average time for all the experts was well over six seconds.[73] Liebeler reasoned that if the experts, firing under far more favorable conditions than

Oswald did, failed most of the time to fire three shots in 5.6 seconds, the shots could hardly be called "easy shots."[74]

Liebeler stated that it was "simply dishonest" not to mention the problem with the sight in the chapter.[75] The telescopic sight, it will be recalled, was defective; thus, if the assassin had placed the crosshairs of the sight on the target, the bullet would have missed. Despite the difficulties this would present in rapid-fire shooting, the chapter neglected to mention the problem.

The chapter asserted that Oswald had sufficient proficiency with a rifle to have committed the assassination.[76] This conclusion was based mainly on the rifle scores Oswald had achieved in the United States Marine Corps. Oswald had taken only two tests. In his first test he scored 212, which was considered by the Marine Corps a "fairly good shot"; in his second test, in 1959, he scored 191, which was considered a "rather poor shot."[77]

On the basis of these scores, Major Anderson and Sergeant Zahm—neither of whom had any direct knowledge of Oswald's training or rifle proficiency—testified that "Oswald was a good shot."[78] The chapter again relied on the testimony of these two witnesses for the conclusion that Oswald was a good shot.[79]

Liebeler, however, stated that "this was the worst kind of selection" because it omitted other witnesses who had had direct experience with Oswald's marksmanship.[80] One such witness was Nelson Delgado, who had stood next to Oswald when he had fired a rifle in the Marine Corps on a number of occasions.[81] Delgado testified that Oswald was a poor shot and often missed the target completely. In fact, according to Delgado, Oswald's targets were considered "a pretty big joke, because he got a lot of 'Maggies drawers' [complete misses]."[82] Both Oswald's rifle score in 1959 (191) and Delgado's testimony indicate that Oswald was a poor, rather than a good, shot. Yet the chapter omitted Delgado's testimony and thus was able to maintain that the 1959 rifle tests were taken under poor conditions and that Oswald was a good shot.

Furthermore, the chapter implied that, while in the Soviet Union, Oswald had practiced his marksmanship by participating in hunts.[83] Liebeler stated, however, that there was no evidence that Oswald had thereby improved his proficiency.[84] In fact, there was information indicating that "Oswald was an *extremely poor* shot and it was necessary for persons who accompanied him on hunts to provide him with game."[85] This information came from the Soviet KGB file on Oswald (furnished by Yuri I. Nossenko, a Soviet intelligence staff officer who defected in February 1964).[86] Although this file casts light on Oswald's rifle proficiency in the Soviet Union, it was never published or referred to by the Commission.

After Oswald returned from the Soviet Union in 1962 there was no evidence that he ever fired a rifle again, except for one time when hunting with his brother. There is also the possibility that Oswald attempted to shoot General Walker. However, the sniper missed Walker, a stationary, well-lit target, at relatively close range.

Thus all evidence of Oswald's rifle proficiency, from his 1959 Marine marksmanship test to his alleged attempted assassination of General Walker, indicates that Oswald was a poor shot. Furthermore, the Commission found no evidence that Oswald had ever practiced firing the rifle.

Liebeler said that the chapter glossed over the evidence that Oswald was a poor shot and had accomplished a difficult feat, and created a "fairy tale" that Oswald was a good shot and had accomplished an "easy shot."[87]

On September 6, 1964, Liebeler submitted his twenty-six-page memorandum to Rankin. At first, Rankin refused to accept the memorandum, saying, "No more memorandums!

The Report has to be published!"[88] However, Liebeler was insistent, and finally Rankin read the memorandum and then immediately summoned Redlich to Washington.[89]

According to Liebeler, Redlich heatedly objected to all Liebeler's criticisms.[90] He explained that he had written the chapter exactly the way the Commission wanted it written.[91] He said, "The Commission judged it an easy shot, and *I* work for the Commission."[92]

Finally Rankin adjudicated the dispute point by point.[93] Most of Liebeler's criticisms were rejected, but some changes were made in the chapter. The problem with the sights was inserted in the chapter, although it was also suggested that the defective sights were actually an advantage for the sniper.[94] The fiber evidence, which had been used to indicate that Oswald had brought the rifle into the Texas Book Depository, and the fingerprint evidence, which had been used to show Oswald's presence at the window, were both assigned only probative value.[95] And the statement that the rifle was in the Paines' home the night before the assassination was made less definite, although the chapter still implied that this was a known fact.[96]

Although Chapter IV is not a "prosecutor's brief" in the sense that it presents only one side of the case, it certainly is not an impartial presentation of the facts. In the final analysis, Redlich did "work for the Commission." That he is a man of high personal integrity only adds to the poignancy of the situation. In his role as editor, he had to select evidence that supported the Commission's judgments. As contradictory evidence and inconsistent details therefore tended to be omitted, the selection process tended to make the Commission's judgments self-reinforcing.

10

The Commission's Conclusions

As COMMISSIONER FORD put it, "Conclusions were the work of the Commission."[1] The staff conducted the investigation and drafted the report, but in the final analysis the Commission had to reach the conclusions and take the responsibility for them. There were five main conclusions.

First, the Commission concluded that the shots came from the Texas School Book Depository. This conclusion was based on medical evidence which showed that at least two of the shots came from the general direction of the Depository; on the testimony of eyewitnesses who saw a rifle in the sixth-floor window of the Depository; and on the fact that the murder weapon and three cartridge cases were found on the sixth floor of the Depository.[2] Although this evidence in itself did not exclude the possibility that other shots came from a different source, it constituted ample proof that shots had come from the Depository.

The second conclusion concerned the sequence of events and presented a difficult problem. It will be recalled that the film of the assassination showed that the President and Governor Connally were hit less than two seconds apart, and that rifle tests showed that it was physically impossible for the murder weapon to be accurately fired twice within this period of time. Thus, either both men were hit by the same bullet or there had to be two assassins. Norman Redlich, Arlen Specter, and other members of the staff took the position that the Report had to conclude that both men were hit by the same bullet.[3] There was, however, no substantial evidence which supported this contention, and there was evidence that all but precluded the possibility that both men had been hit by the same bullet.[4]

The Commission was thus confronted with a dilemma. If it disregarded the evidence that Connally could not have been hit by the same bullet that hit Kennedy, and if it concluded that both men were hit by the same bullet, the credibility of the entire Report might be jeopardized. If, however, the Commission concluded that both men were hit by separate bullets, the single-assassin theory would be untenable in terms of the established evidence and assumptions.

In the "spectrum of opinion" that existed on this question, Ford said he was closest to the position that both men were hit by the same bullet, and Senator Russell was furthest away.[5] In fact, Russell reportedly said that he would not sign a Report which concluded that both men were hit by the same bullet.[6] Senator Cooper and Representative Boggs tended to agree with Russell's position. Cooper said, "I, too, objected to such a conclusion; there was no evidence to show both men were hit by the same bullet."[7] Boggs said, "I had strong doubts about it [the single-bullet theory]," and he added that he felt the question was never resolved.[8]

Both Dulles and McCloy said that they believed the most reasonable explanation of the assassination was that both men were hit by the same bullet.[9] The Commission was thus more or less evenly split on this question, with Ford, Dulles, and McCloy tending toward the conclusion that both men were hit by the same bullet, and Russell, Cooper, and Boggs tending toward the conclusion that both men were hit by separate bullets.

McCloy said that it was of vital importance to have a unanimous Report. He proposed, as a compromise, stating merely that there was evidence that both men were hit by the same bullet but that, in view of other evidence, the Commission could not decide on the probability of this.[10]

There then followed what was described as "the battle of the adjectives."[11] Ford wanted to state that there was "compelling" evidence that both men were hit by the same bullet, while Russell wanted to state merely that there was only "credible" evidence.[12] McCloy finally suggested that the adjective "persuasive" be used, and this word was agreed upon.[13] The Report states:

> Although it is not necessary to any essential findings of the Commission to determine just which shot hit Governor Connally, there is very persuasive evidence from the experts to indicate that the same bullet which pierced the President's throat also caused Governor Connally's wounds. However, Governor Connally's testimony and certain other factors have given rise to some difference of opinion as to this probability but there is no question in the mind of any member of the Commission that all the shots which caused the President's and Governor Con-

nally's wounds were fired from the sixth floor window of the Texas School Book Depository.[14]

The question was thus left open by the Commission.

Third, the Commission concluded that the assassin was Lee Harvey Oswald. This conclusion was based on seven subconclusions: (1) the murder weapon belonged to Oswald; (2) Oswald carried the weapon into the Depository; (3) at the time of the assassination Oswald was at the window from which the shots were fired; (4) the murder weapon was found in the Depository after the assassination; (5) Oswald possessed enough proficiency with a rifle to have committed the assassination; (6) Oswald lied to the police; and (7) Oswald had attempted to kill General Walker.[15]

The most compelling of these subconclusions was that Oswald's rifle was used in the assassination. This fact, together with evidence that Oswald had had the opportunity to commit the assassination, made for a strong case against Oswald. The only other possibility is that another person used Oswald's rifle, but Oswald's subsequent actions—leaving the scene, shooting a policeman, and resisting arrest—certainly were not the actions of an innocent person.

The other subconclusions, however, were based on less substantial evidence. Subconclusion (2)—that Oswald carried the rifle into the Depository—was no more than a plausible assumption;[16] (3)—Oswald's presence at the window—was supported only by "probative" evidence (e.g., Brennan's identification); (4)—the presence of the rifle in the building—merely reinforced (1); (5)—Oswald's rifle capabilities—was based on extremely dubious evidence;[17] (6)—that Oswald lied to the police—had little value as evidence since, purportedly, no record of Oswald's interrogation statements was kept; and (7)—Oswald's attempt to kill Walker—was based mainly on the testimony of Marina Oswald.

The Commission's fourth conclusion concerned Oswald's motive. Although the Commission "could not make any definitive determination of Oswald's motives," it listed five factors "which might have influenced Oswald's decision to assassinate President Kennedy."[18] These possible motives were: (1) Oswald's resentment of all authority; (2) his inability to enter into meaningful relationships with people; (3) his urge to find a place in history; (4) his capacity for violence; and (5) his commitment to Marxism and communism.[19]

Wesley Liebeler, who originally wrote the chapter on Oswald's motivation, said that each Commissioner had his own "pet theory" to explain Oswald's actions.[20] For example, McCloy persistently suggested the "killer-instinct theory" to Liebeler, although support for this theory was not evident in Oswald's life history. Finally this theory was worked into the conclusions as factor (4).[21] Ford insisted that Oswald's commitment to communism be listed as a factor (5),[22] although it was not clear how this commitment had contributed to Oswald's decision. A number of Commissioners felt that Oswald was motivated by an "urge to find a place in history," but the only evidence for this theory was Marina Oswald's February testimony, and in her September testimony Mrs. Oswald refuted her own earlier testimony on this point.[23] Nor were factors (1) and (2) based on objective evidence.

Joseph Ball commented that the Commission replaced Liebeler's informed and brilliant analysis of Oswald's personality with "clichés that belonged in a television script."[24]

Finally there was the question of whether or not Oswald acted alone. Ford said that the draft of the Conclusion stated categorically that there was no conspiracy, but he had insisted that this wording be changed to read: "The Commission has found no evidence of a conspiracy."[25] McCloy said that the Commission could render a conclusion only on the basis of the evidence brought before it,[26] and thus the following qualification was added:

> Because of the difficulty of proving a negative to a certainty the possibility of others being involved with either Oswald or Ruby cannot be rejected categorically, but if there is any such evidence it has been beyond the reach of all investigative agencies and resources of the United States and has not come to the attention of this Commission.[27]

It is true that the Commission found no evidence that others were involved with Oswald in the assassination, but, as has been shown, the investigation was by no means exhaustive or even thorough.[28] The question thus remains: How far did the Commission go in approaching the threshold question of a second assassin?

The Zapruder film shows that the assassination could have been committed by one man alone only under one condition: that Kennedy and Connally were hit by the same bullet. However, the FBI Summary and Supplemental Reports' statements on the autopsy, if accurate, preclude this condition. (They state, it will be recalled, that the first bullet did not exit from the front of the President's body.)[29] Furthermore, even if the Summary and the Supplemental Reports are inaccurate, other evidence arose which showed that it was not possible that both men were hit by the same bullet.[30] Unless the basic facts and assumption established by the Commission are incorrect, there is a strong case that Oswald could not have acted alone.

Why did the Commission fail to take cognizance in its conclusions of this evidence of a second assassin? Quite clearly, a serious discussion of this problem would in itself have undermined the dominant purpose of the Commission, namely, the settling of doubts and suspicions. Indeed, if the Commission had made it clear that very substantial evidence indicated the presence of a second assassin, it would have opened a Pandora's box of doubts and suspicions. In establishing its version of the truth, the Warren Commission acted to reassure the nation and protect the national interest.

Appendices

IMMEDIATELY AFTER the assassination President Johnson ordered the FBI to conduct a full investigation into the tragedy and report its findings to him. One week later, on November 29, 1963, the President appointed the Warren Commission and gave it full responsibility for the investigation. On December 9 the FBI submitted to the Commission a summary report of its investigation to date.

This report, entitled *Investigation of Assassination of President John F. Kennedy, November 22, 1963*, consists of four spiral-bound volumes with J. Edgar Hoover's name and the FBI seal imprinted on the blue covers. The first volume contains the text of the report; in the other three volumes are supporting exhibits (mostly photographs and letters). On January 13, 1964, a fifth and final volume was submitted to the Commission. This volume contains additional information and exhibits.

In the text of this book these first and fifth volumes are referred to as the FBI Summary Report and the FBI Supplemental Report, respectively. Appendix A is a reproduction of the Preface, complete table of contents, and Parts I and II of the first volume of the December 9 report. Similarly, Appendix B consists of the complete table of contents, preface, and Part One of the January 13 volume. Virtually all the biographical material on Oswald in these FBI reports is included in the Warren Report and in its accompanying twenty-six volumes of testimony and exhibits. It is therefore not reproduced here.

APPENDIX A

FBI Summary Report

DECEMBER 9, 1963
(Partial text)

INVESTIGATION OF ASSASSINATION

OF

PRESIDENT JOHN F. KENNEDY

NOVEMBER 22, 1963

PREFACE

Part I briefly relates the assassination of the President and the identification of Oswald as his slayer.

Part II sets forth the evidence conclusively showing that Oswald did assassinate the President.

Part III is in two sections. The first sets forth what the FBI knew about Oswald prior to the assassination; and the second section sets forth the results of our investigation of Oswald's background, activities, associates, et cetera, subsequent to the assassination.

Three sets of exhibits accompany this report. The first sets out evidence tying in Oswald with the assassination of the President; the other two set out documents relative to Oswald's contacts with the Soviets, the Communist Party, et cetera.

We are continuing to receive leads concerning Oswald and, consequently, at the conclusion of the report, it is stated this investigation will continue in order to resolve them.

TABLE OF CONTENTS

I. THE ASSASSINATION

President John Fitzgerald Kennedy was assassinated in Dallas, Texas, at approximately 12:29 p.m. (CST) on November 22, 1963. At the time, the President was en route from Love Field to the Trade Mart in Dallas to address a luncheon sponsored by several civic groups. Among those in the motorcade with the President were his wife, Vice President and Mrs. Lyndon B. Johnson, and Texas Governor John B. Connally and his wife.

A. Assassin in Building

As the motorcade was traveling through downtown Dallas on Elm Street about fifty yards west of the intersection with Houston Street (Exhibit 1), three shots rang out. Two bullets struck President Kennedy, and one wounded Governor Connally. The President, who slumped forward in the car, was rushed to Parkland Memorial Hospital, where he was pronounced dead at 1:00 p.m.

Eyewitnesses at the scene of the shooting saw an individual holding a rifle in a sixth-floor window of the Texas School Book Depository Building located on the corner of Houston and Elm Streets. One individual stated that after he heard what he believed to be a second shot, he looked up, and saw this man take deliberate aim with a rifle and fire in the direction of the Presidential motorcade as it passed. (Exhibit 2)

B. Patrolman Tippit Killed

An immediate investigation was launched to identify and apprehend the President's assailant. Within the hour, at approximately 1:15 p.m., Dallas Patrolman J. D. Tippit, presumably acting on the basis of a broadcast over the police radio, stopped a possible suspect on Tenth Street just east of Patton Street. The man drew a gun and shot Patrolman Tippit three times, resulting in the officer's death. (Exhibit 1) The assailant, subsequently identified as Lee Harvey Oswald, was apprehended in the Texas Theater, 231 West Jefferson Boulevard. (Exhibit 1) In the course of the apprehension, which took place about 2:00 p.m., he resisted violently and attempted to shoot still another police officer.

Identified as an employee in the building from which the shots were fired at President Kennedy and Governor Connally, Oswald became a prime suspect in the assassination of President Kennedy. However, when interviewed following his apprehension, Oswald denied any knowledge of or participation in the assassination of the President or Tippit's murder.

Nevertheless, evidence developed in the investigation points conclusively to the assassination of President Kennedy by Lee Harvey Oswald, avowed Marxist, a former defector to the Soviet Union and the self-appointed Secretary of the New Orleans Chapter of the Fair Play for Cuba Committee, a pro-Castro organization.

Oswald, aged 24, attended schools in New Orleans, Louisiana, Fort Worth, Texas, and New York, New York, and served in the U. S. Marine Corps from 1956 to 1959, during which time he qualified as a sharpshooter. In 1959 he traveled to the Soviet Union where he was employed for approximately three years as a factory worker. He publicly announced his intention of becoming a Russian citizen, but apparently changed his mind and returned to the United States in 1962 with a Russian wife and a child. A second child has since been born. Subsequent to his return, he was employed for brief periods in New Orleans, Louisiana, and Dallas, Texas.

II.   THE EVIDENCE

A.   Events Prior to the Assassination

Lee Harvey Oswald, using the name O. H. Lee, rented a furnished room at 1026 North Beckley Street in Dallas, Texas, on October 14, 1963. He used the room during the week and, on weekends, traveled to Irving, Texas, where his wife and children resided. He had made arrangements with a fellow employee, Buell W. Frazier, to drive him to Irving every Friday night and normally returned with Mr. Frazier to Dallas every Monday morning.

On Thursday evening, November 21, 1963, Oswald departed from his customary schedule of travel to Irving. Claiming to Mr. Frazier that he wanted to obtain some curtain rods for his room from Mrs. Ruth Paine, his landlady in Irving, he arranged to ride with Mr. Frazier to Irving that night. It is the only known instance in which Oswald departed from his practice of making the trip on other than a weekend.

Mrs. Ruth Paine, 2515 West Fifth Street, landlady at the residence in which Oswald's wife resided in Irving, said that Oswald made no mention of curtain rods to her on the evening of November 21, 1963, nor did she plan to give him any curtain rods. But Oswald's wife, Marina, has revealed that her husband owned a rifle which he kept wrapped in a blanket in the garage at the Irving residence. She said he spent the night of November 21, 1963, with her and left early the following morning before she had awakened. On November 22, 1963, she noticed that the blanket in which the rifle had been wrapped was still in the garage, but the rifle was gone.

Subsequent to the assassination, the blanket was examined at the FBI Laboratory. Body hairs located on it were found to match in microscopic characteristics the body hairs of Lee Harvey Oswald. (Exhibit 3)

When Oswald left Irving, Texas, on the morning of November 22, 1963, he carried a long package wrapped in brown paper. Mr. Frazier, with whom he customarily rode, described it as a "kind of sack that one obtains in a five-and-ten-cent store." Oswald told him it contained curtain rods. On arrival in Dallas, Mr. Frazier, after parking his car, saw Oswald enter the Texas School Book Depository Building carrying the package. After the assassination of President Kennedy, brown wrapping paper in the shape of a long bag was found near the window from which the shots were fired on the sixth floor of the Depository Building. (Exhibit 4)

A latent fingerprint developed by the FBI Identification Division on the long paper bag was determined to be identical with the left index fingerprint impression of Lee Harvey Oswald. (Exhibit 5)

- 5 -

A latent palm print developed on the same paper was identified as being identical with the right palm print of Oswald. (Exhibit 6)

Mr. Frazier, after viewing the long brown paper bag found on the sixth floor of the Texas School Book Depository Building, could not definitely state whether the bag was the one observed by him in Oswald's possession on the morning of November 22, 1963. Mr. Frazier's sister, Mrs. Linnie May Randle, examined the bag and advised that it could have been the long paper bag she saw Oswald place in her brother's car on that morning as they departed for work.

In addition to having been seen by Mr. Frazier entering the building with a brown paper package the morning of the assassination, Oswald was seen in the building later that morning by several fellow employees. Between 11:30 and 12:00 noon, Oswald was observed on the fifth floor by three employees. During this period, he requested one of the employees, Charles D. Givens, who was descending in the elevator, to close the elevator gates when he got off so he, Oswald, could summon the elevator to the sixth floor.

B. Events Following the Assassination

Oswald's Movements

In the search that was initiated within the Texas School Book Depository Building by the police immediately after the assassination,

Oswald was determined to be still on the premises. He was seen
by Roy S. Truly, Warehouse Superintendent, and a police officer in
a small lunchroom on the second floor. (Exhibit 7) He was not
questioned at the time inasmuch as Mr. Truly identified him to the
officer as an employee of the building. Shortly thereafter, Mr. Truly
accounted for the whereabouts of all of his employees except Oswald
and so advised the police.

Identified on Bus

A short time later, Oswald was observed by his former landlady, Mrs. Mary E. Bledsoe, 621 North Marsalis Avenue, boarding
a city bus about seven blocks from the scene of the assassination.
(Exhibit 1) Mrs. Bledsoe, who was riding on the bus, stated that he
appeared to be somewhat nervous. She also noted that Oswald was
wearing dirty clothing, a marked change from his usual neat appearance.

Cecil J. McWatters, the driver of the bus, selected Oswald
from a police line-up as resembling a passenger who entered his bus
on November 22, 1963, in the general vicinity of the assassination.
Mr. McWatters was unable to definitely establish the time or place
where Oswald boarded the bus but recalled that it was shortly after
the assassination. He remembered commenting to this passenger,
"I wonder where they shot the President." He said the passenger
replied, "They shot him in the temple."

Mr. McWatters also identified a bus transfer in Oswald's possession at the time of his apprehension as one he had issued on November 22, 1963.

Mrs. Bledsoe stated that Oswald traveled less than two blocks on the bus. She pointed out that traffic had become congested and a motorist alongside commented to the bus driver that the President had been shot. Mrs. Bledsoe said Oswald left the bus and disappeared in the crowd.

In a Taxicab

William W. Whaley, a taxicab driver, positively identified Oswald in a police line-up on November 23, 1963, at the Dallas Police Department as a passenger in his cab on November 22, 1963. He was unable to remember the exact time, but was certain he picked up Oswald between 12:30 and 12:45 p. m. at the Greyhound Bus Terminal Taxi Stand, approximately seven blocks from the scene of the assassination (Exhibit 1), and transported him about two and three quarter miles to the 500 block of North Beckley Street in Dallas (Exhibit 1). As previously noted, the room rented by Oswald was at 1026 North Beckley Street.

Arrival at Room

Mrs. Earlene Roberts, housekeeper at 1026 North Beckley Street, positively identified Oswald as the man who had rented the

room from her on October 14, 1963, under the name O. H. Lee.
She said Oswald came home shortly after she heard the news that
the President had been shot. She estimated the time as approximately
1:00 p. m. He obtained a jacket from his room and left hurriedly. She
also said that while she had never observed Oswald in possession of
a gun, she noticed a holster for a hand gun in his room late on the
afternoon of November 22, 1963.

Oswald's Murder of Patrolman Tippit

At about 1:15 p. m. on November 22, 1963, a taxicab driver,
W. W. Scoggins, observed a uniformed police officer (Patrolman
J. D. Tippit) talking to a man alongside the officer's police vehicle
at 10th Street just east of Patton Street. The driver said he heard
a gun firing and saw the officer fall beside the police car. (Exhibit 1)
His assailant ran west on 10th Street, south on Patton Street, and
then west on Jefferson Boulevard.

Eyewitnesses to Tippit's Killing

On November 23, 1963, this same taxi driver identified Oswald
at a police line-up as Officer Tippit's assailant. Another eyewitness
to the killing identified Lee Harvey Oswald as the assailant who drew
a hand gun from inside his shirt and shot Tippit.

- 9 -

C.   Oswald's Apprehension

Acting on information from a police radio broadcast reporting that a suspect in the killing of a police officer was seen entering the Texas Theater, 231 West Jefferson Boulevard, Dallas police apprehended Oswald at about 2:00 p. m. , in the theater. (Exhibit 1) One of the officers took a . 38 Special revolver out of Oswald's right hand. (Exhibit 8)

Gun Misfired

One of the arresting officers stated that when Oswald was first approached in the theater he attempted to pull a revolver from his shirt. In the ensuing struggle with the police officer, Oswald pulled the trigger but the gun did not fire. An examination of this gun confirmed that one of the six cartridges taken from the weapon had a hammer indentation on the primer but had not fired.

Revolver Traced to Oswald

FBI investigation determined that the . 38 Special Smith and Wesson revolver, serial number V510210, taken from Lee Harvey Oswald was shipped on March 20, 1963, from George Rose and Company, Incorporated, Los Angeles, California, to A. J. Hidell, Post Office Box 2915, Dallas, Texas. The cost of the weapon was $29. 95. Examination by the FBI Laboratory determined that the writing on the mail order coupon used in the purchase of this weapon was written by Lee Harvey Oswald.

- 10 -

Four cartridge cases found in the immediate vicinity of the shooting of Officer Tippit on November 22, 1963, were furnished to the FBI by Dallas police. An examination of these cartridge cases by the FBI Laboratory determined that they had been fired in Oswald's .38 Special Smith and Wesson revolver.

D. Interview of the Assassin

Lee Harvey Oswald, upon interview after his apprehension on November 22, 1963, admitted that he had been living at 1026 North Beckley Street, Dallas, Texas, under the name of O. H. Lee. He also admitted that he was in the Texas School Book Depository Building where he was employed, on November 22, 1963. Oswald claimed, however, that he was on the first floor of the building when the Presidential motorcade passed. Following the shooting of the President, he said he believed that there would be no further work performed and he decided to go home. He said he went to his Dallas residence, changed his clothes, and then went to a movie.

Oswald admitted he carried a gun with him to the movie and stated that he did this because he "felt like it." He offered no other explanation. Oswald denied that he ever ordered, owned or possessed a rifle. However, in a subsequent search of Oswald's residence in Irving, Texas, by officers of the Dallas Police Department, a photograph

- 11 -

was found showing Oswald wearing a sidearm and holding a rifle.
(Exhibit 9) The rifle in the photograph is similar in appearance to the
6. 5 millimeter, bolt-action rifle which, as will be shown, had been
previously purchased by Oswald. Oswald, upon interview, also
denied bringing any package to work with him on the morning of
November 22, 1963.

Included in his personal effects at the time of Oswald's arrest
were a Selective Service card (Exhibit 10) in the name of Alek James
Hidell and a card issued to Lee H. Oswald dated May 28, 1963, by the
Fair Play for Cuba Committee. (Exhibit 11) Oswald said that he had
been secretary of the New Orleans Chapter of the Fair Play for Cuba
Committee. Oswald refused to discuss the Selective Service card in
his possession. Examination in the FBI Laboratory determined that
the Selective Service card is fraudulent and counterfeit.

Oswald stated he had never been in Mexico except to visit
Tijuana on one occasion (date not furnished). He admitted having
resided in the Soviet Union for three years where he had many friends.

When a Special Agent of the FBI sought to obtain a physical
description and background data from Oswald, the latter commented:
"I know your tactics; there is a similar agency in Russia. You are
using the soft touch and, of course, the procedure in Russia would be
quite different. "

In accounting for his activities on the afternoon of November 22, 1963, Oswald stated he was on the second floor of the Texas School Book Depository Building at the time the building was searched. He stated Mr. Truly, the building superintendent, and a police officer entered the room and Mr. Truly identified Oswald to the officer as an employee. Oswald related that he then took the Coca-Cola which he had just purchased to the first floor, where he stood around and then had lunch in the employees' lunchroom on the second floor. Thereafter, he stated, he went outside the building, stood around for five to ten minutes, and then went home because he did not believe there was going to be any more work that day due to the confusion in the building. Oswald advised that following arrival at his residence he left to attend a movie where he was apprehended by the Dallas police.

On subsequent interview on November 23, 1963, Oswald denied telling Mr. Frazier that the purpose of his visit to Irving, Texas, on the night of November 21, 1963, was to obtain some curtain rods from Mrs. Ruth Paine.

Oswald stated information previously furnished by him to the effect that he rode a bus from his place of employment to his residence on November 22, 1963, was not entirely true. On this latter interview Oswald stated he did board a city bus at his place of employment but after riding a block or two he left the bus due to the traffic congestion and took a city cab to his apartment on North Beckley Street. Oswald stated that after arriving at his apartment he changed his shirt and trousers because they were dirty.

Oswald denied that he had kept a rifle in the garage at Mrs. Paine's residence in Irving, Texas, but stated he did have some property, including two sea bags and a couple of suitcases, stored there.

Oswald denied that he was a member of the Communist Party and stated he had nothing against President Kennedy personally. He stated, however, that in view of the charges against him he did not desire to discuss the matter further. Oswald denied shooting President Kennedy and added that he was not aware of the fact that Governor John Connally had also been shot.

The photograph of Oswald holding a rifle and wearing a holstered pistol was exhibited to him and Oswald stated he would not discuss the photograph. Oswald stated the head of the individual in the photograph could be his but it was entirely possible that the police department had superimposed this part of the photograph over the body of someone else.

E. The Assassination Weapon

During the police search of the Texas School Book Depository Building, a rifle of Italian manufacture was found between some boxes on the sixth floor near the northwest or opposite corner of the building from which the fatal shots were fired. On examination, it was determined to be a 6.5 millimeter Mannlicher-Carcano, bolt-action, clip-fed rifle, serial number C 2766, equipped with a four-power telescopic sight of Japanese manufacture. (Exhibit 12)

A diagram of the sixth floor of the Texas School Book Depository Building shows the location of the window from which the fatal shots were fired and shows the location where the rifle was found by Dallas police officers. (Exhibit 13)

A photograph of the rifle and of the blanket and long brown paper bag previously referred to is included showing the relative size of each. (Exhibit 14)

Rifle Ordered by Oswald

FBI investigation determined that this rifle was part of a shipment of surplus Italian military weapons purchased for resale in the United States by Klein's Sporting Goods, Chicago, Illinois. The company's records disclose that the rifle, identified by serial number C 2766, was shipped, with rifle scope mounted, on March 20, 1963, by parcel post to A. Hidell, Post Office Box 2915, Dallas, Texas. (Exhibit 15) The gun was ordered by airmail and the envelope was postmarked March 12, 1963, at Dallas. Payment was made by U. S. Postal Money Order 2, 202, 130, 462 in the amount of $21. 45, issued at Dallas, Texas,

- 15 -

March 12, 1963, payable to Klein's Sporting Goods. It was signed by
A. Hidell, Post Office Box 2915, Dallas, Texas. Post Office Box 2915
had been rented on October 9, 1962, through an application signed by
Lee H. Oswald and was relinquished on May 14, 1963. The FBI
Laboratory conducted handwriting examinations based on known
handwriting specimens of Oswald's from a 1963 passport application
(Exhibit 16) and from a letter dated January 30, 1961, which he sent
to John B. Connally, now the Governor of Texas, formerly Secretary
of the Navy. (Exhibit 17)

The FBI Laboratory examination of the handwriting on the
envelope addressed to Klein's Sporting Goods, in which the rifle order
was contained, determined that the envelope was addressed by Oswald.
(Exhibit 18)

The examination by the FBI Laboratory of the hand printing
appearing on the above order form for the rifle determined that it was
prepared by Oswald. (Exhibit 18)

The handwriting on the money order issued in payment for the
rifle was determined by the FBI Laboratory to have been prepared by
Oswald. (Exhibit 19)

It was determined by the FBI Laboratory examination that the
handwriting on the application for Post Office Box 2915 was prepared
by Oswald. (Exhibit 20)

- 16 -

It should be noted that the above rifle was sent to Oswald, using the alias A. J. Hidell, at Post Office Box 2915 in Dallas, on the same date that the revolver previously referred to as having killed Officer Tippit was shipped to him from Los Angeles.

Tests of Rifle

By actual tests it has been demonstrated by the FBI that a skilled person can fire three accurately aimed shots with this weapon in five seconds.

Textile Examination

When apprehended, Oswald was wearing a long-sleeved, multi-colored sport shirt. A small tuft of textile fibers was found adhering to a jagged area on the left side of the metal butt plate of the rifle owned by Oswald. Included in this tuft were gray-black, dark blue, and orange-yellow fibers which the FBI Laboratory determined matched in microscopic characteristics the fibers in the shirt worn by Lee Harvey Oswald. (Exhibit 21)

According to Mrs. Bledsoe, Oswald's former landlady, Oswald was wearing this sport shirt on the bus shortly after the assassination.

Cartridges Fired in Oswald's Rifle

Three empty cartridge cases were found near the window from which the shots were fired on the sixth floor of the building. These cartridge cases were examined by the FBI Laboratory, and it was determined that all three had been fired in the rifle owned by Oswald. (Exhibit 22)

Immediately after President Kennedy and Governor Connally were admitted to Parkland Memorial Hospital, a bullet was found on one of the stretchers. Medical examination of the President's body revealed that one of the bullets had entered just below his shoulder to the right of the spinal column at an angle of 45 to 60 degrees downward, that there was no point of exit, and that the bullet was not in the body. An examination of this bullet by the FBI Laboratory determined that it had been fired from the rifle owned by Oswald. (Exhibit 23)

Bullet fragments found in the automobile in which President Kennedy was riding were examined in the FBI Laboratory. It was definitely established, from markings on two of the fragments, that they had been fired from the rifle owned by Oswald. (Exhibit 24)

Palm Print on Rifle

Dallas police lifted a latent impression off the underside of the gun barrel near the end of the foregrip of the rifle recovered on the

sixth floor of the Texas School Book Depository Building. When the
rifle was properly assembled, this impression was concealed by the
wooden foregrip. This impression has been identified by the FBI
Identification Division as the right palm print of Lee Harvey Oswald.
(Exhibit 25)

F.   Other Evidence
Cardboard Cartons

A latent palm print which was located on a cardboard carton
found by police in the room from which the shots were fired was
identified as the right palm print of Oswald. (Exhibit 26) One latent
fingerprint (Exhibit 27) and latent left palm print (Exhibit 28) developed
on another box from this same room were also identified as Oswald's
impressions.

Paraffin Tests

Following Oswald's apprehension on November 22, 1963,
Dr. M. F. Mason of Dallas concluded, after tests, that paraffin
casts made of Oswald's hands contained traces of nitrate consistent
with the residue on the hands of a person who had recently handled or
fired a firearm.

Photograph

Film which was furnished by spectators at the scene of the
assassination was reviewed. One film shows an object in the window
of the sixth-floor room from which the shots were fired as the President's

car passed the Depository Building.   This object is not susceptible to
identification because of the quality of the picture.   (Exhibit 29)

Map in Oswald's Effects

In the search of Oswald's belongings at his Dallas Beckley Street
room, police found a street map of Dallas and vicinity which bore
markings to indicate particular locations.   (Exhibit 30)   Mrs. Ruth
Paine stated she gave an ENCO map of Dallas and vicinity to Oswald on
October 7, 1963, when he was looking for employment.   While this map
may have been used by Oswald in seeking employment, the significance
of the markings is not known.

G.   Prior Similar Act

Mrs. Marina Oswald was interviewed on December 3, 1963, by the
FBI concerning an undated note which was called to the attention of the FBI
the same day.   According to Mrs. Oswald this note, which was written in
Russian, was found by her one night last spring in a room where her husband
kept his things at their residence at 214 West Neely Street, Dallas.   (Exhibit 31;
English translation, Exhibit 32) On that night, although Oswald told her he
was going to attend a typewriting class at an evening school in Dallas, he
came rushing into the house around midnight very pale and agitated.   Mrs. Oswald
asked what was wrong and he replied that he had tried to kill General Walker
by shooting him with a rifle and he did not know if he had hit him.   At this
time Oswald told her that General Walker was the leader of the fascists in

Dallas and it was necessary to remove him. Mrs. Oswald said she thought the rifle used by her husband to shoot at General Walker and the rifle he kept in Mrs. Paine's garage in Irving, Texas, were one and the same.

Mrs. Oswald said she kept the note written in Russian by Oswald, which was evidently a farewell letter, and threatened Oswald with going to the police with the letter if he ever planned another such "crazy" scheme. She advised that as a result of this incident she insisted that they move from Dallas.

The writing on this note has been identified by the FBI Laboratory as being handwriting of Lee Harvey Oswald.

It is noted that former Major General Edwin A. Walker resides in Dallas and a rifle bullet was shot through the window of his home on April 10, 1963, narrowly missing General Walker. The person firing the shot was never identified.

Investigation showed that Mr. and Mrs. Oswald resided at 214 West Neely Street in Dallas during April, 1963, and left that address on April 24, 1963, when they moved to New Orleans. At that time, in April, 1963, Oswald was renting mail box number 2915 in the main post office on Ervay Street in Dallas, which he relinquished as of May 14, 1963.

In this note, Oswald also mentioned "You and the baby. " In April, 1963, Mrs. Oswald had one child and the second child was born October 20, 1963.

The bullet which was fired into General Walker's house on April 10, 1963, was recovered by the Dallas Police Department. Examination of this bullet by the FBI Laboratory disclosed that while the bullet is extremely distorted and mutilated, it has the general characteristics of those bullets fired from the 6. 5 millimeter Mannlicher-Carcano rifle belonging to Oswald. This rifle was found in the Texas School Book Depository Building following the assassination of President Kennedy. Because of the mutilation of this bullet and because the gun barrel may have changed since April 10, 1963, it was not possible to determine whether or not this bullet was fired from Oswald's rifle.

APPENDIX B

FBI Supplemental Report

JANUARY 13, 1964
(Partial text)

INVESTIGATION OF ASSASSINATION

OF PRESIDENT JOHN F. KENNEDY

NOVEMBER 22, 1963

SUPPLEMENTAL REPORT

JANUARY 13, 1964

PREFACE

Part One of this Supplemental Report sets forth additional evidence developed incriminating Lee Harvey Oswald in the assassination of President John F. Kennedy.

Part Two of this Supplemental Report sets forth additional information developed regarding Lee Harvey Oswald.

Part Three of this Supplemental Report contains additional exhibits.

TABLE OF CONTENTS

PART ONE: <u>ADDITIONAL INFORMATION PERTAINING TO THE ASSASSINATION</u>

I. FBI Laboratory Examinations

A. President's Clothing

The FBI Laboratory has determined that the bullets used
in the assassination of President Kennedy on November 22, 1963,
were a military type manufactured by the Western Cartridge
Company, East Alton, Illinois. These bullets have solid noses
with full copper alloy jackets and lead cores. Examination of
the President's clothing by the FBI Laboratory disclosed that
there was a small hole in the back of his coat and shirt
approximately six inches below the top of the collar and two
inches to the right of the middle seam of the coat. There
were minute traces of copper on the fabric surrounding the hole.
Medical examination of the President's body had revealed that
the bullet which entered his back had penetrated to a distance
of less than a finger length.   (Exhibits 59 and 60)

There is a slit approximately one-half inch long about
one inch below the collar button in the overlap of the shirt the
President was wearing. The slit has the characteristics of an
exit hole for a projectile. There is also a nick on the left
side of the tie knot, which possibly was caused by the same
projectile as it passed through the shirt. The coat and shirt
were X-rayed for metal bullet fragments that might have been
embedded among the layers of the fabric, but none were found.
The Chief Pathologist at Bethesda Naval Hospital had advised
that the projectile which had entered the President's skull

region had disintegrated into at least 40 particles of bullet fragments as shown by the number located.

All of the clothing and items submitted were examined by the FBI Laboratory for other pertinent evidence, but none was found.

B. __Photographs__

A motion picture of the assassination taken by an amateur photographer, Abraham Zapruder, 3909 Marquette Street, Dallas, was examined by the FBI Laboratory. The best estimate of the time interval of the shots fired is that approximately six seconds elapsed from the first to the final shot, with the second shot occurring approximately in the middle of the six-second period. The firing period begins with the first shot, so that it is necessary to operate the rifle bolt only twice to fire three shots within a given period of time. The assassination weapon is a right-handed, bolt-action, military rifle. Oswald's wife has stated that Lee Oswald was right-handed.

The photograph showing an object in the window of the sixth floor room from which the shots were fired (described on pages 19-20 of the initial report) has been examined by both the FBI Laboratory and the United States Navy Photographic Interpretation Center, Suitland, Maryland. From a study of this and other photographs in the sequence, neither the FBI Laboratory nor the Navy Photographic Interpretation Center

- 3 -

could make a positive determination of what the object is.
It was concluded, however, that the image seen does not
depict the form of a person or persons and is possibly a
stack of boxes later determined to have been in the room.

When Oswald was interviewed on November 23, 1963,
regarding the photograph which portrays him holding a rifle and
wearing a holstered pistol, he would not discuss the photograph
without the advice of an attorney. He admitted that the head
of the individual in the photograph could be his but suggested
the possibility that the police had superimposed this part
of the photograph over the body of someone else. However,
Marina Oswald, when questioned regarding this photograph,
stated that she had taken it. (Exhibit 9)

The FBI Laboratory has examined this photograph and has
concluded that, while the rifle in the photograph is similar
in appearance to the assassination weapon and while there are
no apparent differences between them, there is insufficient
detail to identify the rifle in the photograph as the
assassination weapon.

C. Paper Bag

The FBI Laboratory examined the brown wrapping paper in
the shape of a long bag which was found near the window from
which the shots were fired. It was determined that the wrapping
paper and the three-inch manila tape used to construct the bag
were the same as that used by the Texas School Book Depository.

- 4 -

The bag was examined for any evidence of the outline of a rifle but no significant indentations were found. Dismantled, Oswald's rifle will fit into this paper bag.

D. Bullet Fragments

Several tiny fragments of lead were recovered from the President's head and his limousine, and one was recovered from Governor Connally's arm. However, these fragments were too small for the FBI Laboratory to effect an identification with any weapon.

Examination of the limousine also disclosed that the windshield was cracked and there was a dented area in the windshield chrome molding at the top near the center which may have been caused by bullet fragments.

NOTES

INDEX

NOTES

Preface

1. Carl Marcy, *Presidential Commissions*, New York, 1945, pp. 98*ff.*

2. *N.Y. Times,* January 25, 1942, p. 1+ (Report of the Roberts Commission).

3. *N.Y. Times,* December 7, 1962, p. 5.

4. There are some notable exceptions, including: Paul L. Freese, "The Warren Commission and the Fourth Shot: A Reflection on the Fundamentals of Forensic Fact-Finding." *New York University Law Review,* Vol. 40, No. 3, May 1965, pp. 424–65. Also, Dwight Macdonald, "A Critique of the Warren Report," *Esquire,* March 1965, p. 59*ff.*

5. *Report of the President's Commission on the Assassination of President Kennedy* (1964) Washington, D.C. (hereinafter *Report*).

6. *Hearings Before the President's Commission on the Assassination of President Kennedy* (1964) Washington, D.C. (hereinafter *Hearings*). Vols. I–V comprise testimony given before the Commission, Vols. VI–XV comprise testimony given before members of the legal staff of the Commission, Vols. XVI–XXVI comprise exhibits introduced in the testimony.

7. Material from the U.S. National Archives will hereinafter be cited by the Commission Document number

listed in the U.S. National Archives index.

8. The chronological file was made available by Assistant Counsel Wesley J. Liebeler, and will be hereinafter cited as Chronological File.

9. Interview with Senator John Sherman Cooper in Washington, D.C., May 5, 1965 (hereinafter Cooper Interview).

10. Interview with Representative Hale Boggs in Washington, D.C., June 11, 1965 (hereinafter Boggs Interview).

11. Interview with Representative Gerald R. Ford in Washington, D.C., May 5, 1965 (hereinafter Ford Interview).

12. Interview with Allen W. Dulles in Washington, D.C., September 29, 1965 (hereinafter Dulles Interview).

13. Interview with John J. McCloy in New York City, June 7, 1965 (hereinafter McCloy Interview).

14. Interviews with J. Lee Rankin in New York City, March 29, 1965 (hereinafter Rankin Interview I), and September 23, 1965 (hereinafter Rankin Interview II).

15. Interview with Norman Redlich in New York City, March 23, 1965 (hereinafter Redlich Interview).

16. Interview with Howard P. Willens in Washington, D.C., May 3, 1965 (hereinafter Willens Interview).

17. Interview with Alfred Goldberg in Washington, D.C., May 5, 1965 (hereinafter Goldberg Interview).

18. Interview with Francis W. H. Adams in New York City, July 8, 1965 (hereinafter Adams Interview).

19. Interview with Joseph A. Ball in New York City, June 24, 1965 (hereinafter Ball Interview).

20. Interviews with Melvin A. Eisenberg in New York City, March 24, 1965 (hereinafter Eisenberg Interview I), and August 5, 1965 (hereinafter Eisenberg Interview II).

21. Interview with Wesley J. Liebeler in Newfane, Vermont, June 30–July 1, 1965 (hereinafter Liebeler Interview).

22. Interview with Arlen Specter in Philadelphia, Pa., August 25, 1965 (hereinafter Specter Interview).

23. Interview with Samuel A. Stern in Washington, D.C., June 10, 1965 (hereinafter Stern Interview).

1. Overview: The Ten-Month Investigation

1. *Texas Supplemental Report on the Assassination of President John F. Kennedy and the Serious Wounding of Governor John B. Connally*, pp. 1, 8, 20, Austin, Texas, 1964 (hereinafter *Texas Report*).

2. *Report*, Foreword, p. x (1964), Washington, D.C.

3. *Ibid.*, p. 471 (Executive Order 11130).

4. *Report*, Foreword, p. x.

5. Dulles Interview.

6. *Report*, Foreword, p. x.

7. McCloy Interview.

8. *Ibid.*

9. *Texas Report, op. cit.*, p. 4.

10. *Ibid.*, p. 5.

11. *Ibid.*, p. 6.

12. *Ibid.*

13. Rankin Interview I.

14. *Ibid.*

15. *Ibid.*

16. *Ibid.*

17. Goldberg Interview.

18. *Ibid.*

19. Liebeler Interview.

20. *Report*, Foreword, p. xi. A fifth volume, the Supplemental Report, was submitted on January 13, 1964. See Appendices.

21. Rankin Interview I.

22. McCloy Interview.

23. Rankin Interview II.

24. Dulles Interview.

25. Rankin Interview II.

26. Dulles Interview.

27. *Report*, Foreword, p. xiii.

28. Rankin Interview II.

29. *Report*, Foreword, p. xii.

30. *Ibid.*, p. xiii+.

31. *Ibid.*, p. xii.

32. Willens Interview.

33. *Ibid.*

34. Stern Interview. Also Goldberg Interview.

35. Rankin Interview I.

36. Redlich Interview.

37. Eisenberg Interview I.

38. Rankin Interview I.

39. Redlich Interview.

40. Rankin Interview I. Also Liebeler Interview.

41. Willens Interview.

42. *Report*, p. 476+. Rankin later decided to drop the distinction between "senior" and "junior" lawyers, and all were called "assistant counsel."

43. Liebeler Interview.

44. Rankin Interview I.

45. Rankin Interview I and Willens Interview.

46. Ford Interview.

47. Willens Interview.

48. *Ibid.*

49. Rankin Interview I.

50. Willens Interview.

51. *Ibid.*

52. Liebeler Interview.

53. Adams Interview.

54. Ball Interview.

55. Liebeler Interview.

56. Redlich Interview.

57. *Ibid.*

58. Stern Interview.

59. Willens Interview.

60. *Ibid.*

61. Liebeler Interview.

62. *Ibid.*

63. Rankin Interview I.

64. Liebeler Interview.

65. Dulles Interview.

66. *Report*, Foreword, p. xiii.

67. *Infra*, p. 21

68. *Report*, Foreword, p. xiii+.

69. *Ibid.*, p. xiv.

70. *Hearings*, Vol. XXIV, p. 445.

71. Rankin Interview I.

72. *Report*, p. 501+.

73. Rankin Interview I.

74. Gerald R. Ford and John R. Stiles, *Portrait of the Assassin*, New York, 1965, p. 13.

75. Rankin Interview II.

76. Ford and Stiles, *op. cit.*, p. 14.

77. *Ibid.*

78. *Ibid.*

79. *Ibid.*, p. 25.

80. U.S. National Archives.

81. *Hearings*, Vol. V., p. 141.

82. Specter Interview.
83. Rankin Interview II and Stern Interview.
84. Rankin Interview II.
85. *Ibid.*
86. *Hearings,* Vol. I, pp. 1*ff.*
87. *Infra,* p. 96
88. Eisenberg Interview II.
89. Willens Interview.
90. Ball Interview.
91. Liebeler Interview.
92. *Ibid.*
93. Eisenberg Interview I.
94. Rankin Interview I.
95. *Ibid.*
96. *Report,* Foreword, pp. xiv–xv.
97. Liebeler Interview.
98. Willens Interview.
99. Rankin Interview I.
100. Eisenberg Interview I.
101. Ball Interview.
102. Liebeler Interview.
103. Ball Interview.
104. *Hearings,* Vol. LI, pp. 140–270, *passim.*
105. *Hearings,* Vol. II, p. 33.
106. *Ibid.,* p. 58.
107. Specter Interview.
108. Liebeler Interview.
109. Eisenberg Interview I.
110. Liebeler Interview. Jenner was to do Oswald's preschool life, Ely his education, and Liebeler his military and work record.
111. Interviews with Goldberg, Willens, Ford, Liebeler, Eisenberg.
112. Ball Interview.
113. Liebeler Interview.
114. Eisenberg Interview I.
115. Willens Interview.
116. Rankin Interviews I and II.
117. Liebeler Interview.

118. Ball Interview.
119. Liebeler Interview.
120. Specter Interview.
121. Goldberg Interview.
122. Liebeler Interview.
123. *Ibid.*
124. Specter Interview.
125. Liebeler Interview.
126. Eisenberg Interview II.
127. Rankin Interview II.
128. *Ibid.*
129. Ball Interview.
130. Liebeler Interview.
131. Goldberg Interview.
132. *N.Y. Times,* June 8. 1964, p. 21:4.
133. *N.Y. Times,* June 19, 1964, p. 13:1.
134. *N.Y. Times,* June 30, 1964, p. 2:5.
135. Liebeler Interview.
136. *Ibid.* Eisenberg came for long weekends, and Stern was available when he was needed.
137. Redlich Interview.
138. Goldberg Interview.
139. Liebeler Interview (and unpublished colloquium).
140. Liebeler Interview.
141. Goldberg Interview.
142. Liebeler Interview.
143. Interviews with Dulles, McCloy, Ford, Boggs, and Cooper.
144. Liebeler Interview.
145. *Ibid.*
146. *Report,* Foreword, p. viii.
147. Liebeler Interview. Also Eisenberg Interview I.
148. *Report,* Foreword, p. xv. All the Commission's documents and working papers were committed to the U.S. National Archives.

2. The Dominant Purpose

1. *Report*, p. 471 (Executive Order No. 11130).

2. *Hearings*, Vol. II, p. 34.

3. *354 U.S. 178*, p. 187.

4. Anthony Lewis, "New Look at the Chief Justice," *N.Y. Times Magazine*, p. 9 (January 19, 1964). The fact that this same story was reprinted in the *N.Y. Times* on September 28, 1964 (p. 14:6), indicates that it was never denied.

5. Rankin Interview I.

6. Dulles Interview.

7. McCloy Interview.

8. Cooper Interview.

9. Ford Interview.

10. Ford and Stiles, *op. cit.*, p. 19.

11. *Ibid.*, p. 14, and *Hearings*, Vol. V, p. 242.

12. Ford and Stiles, *op. cit.*, p. 14.

13. *Hearings*, Vol. V, p. 243.

14. *Ibid.*, pp. 242–43, and Rankin Interview II.

15. *Hearings*, Vol. V, p. 112.

16. *Ibid.*, p. 242.

17. Ford and Stiles, *op. cit.*, p. 20.

18. *Ibid.*, p. 15.

19. *Ibid.*, p. 22.

20. *Ibid.*, p. 20.

21. *Ibid.*, p. 19.

22. *Ibid.*

23. *Ibid.*, p. 21.

24. *Ibid.*

25. *Ibid.*, p. 22.

26. *Ibid.*, p. 24.

27. *Ibid.*, p. 23.

28. *Ibid.*, p. 24.

29. *N.Y. Times*, February 5, 1964, p. 19:1.

30. *Hearings*, Vol. XVII, p. 814.

31. *Ibid.*, pp. 815–18.

32. *Ibid.*, p. 741 and Commission Exhibit 825 (*ibid.*) Warren De Bruey, the FBI agent who allegedly threatened to send an undercover agent to infiltrate the same small New Orleans anti-Castro organization which Oswald later attempted to infiltrate, did *not* submit an affidavit. (Vol. X, pp. 33 *ff.*)

33. *Ibid.*, p. 803.

34. *Hearings*, Vol. V, p. 112. The Commission was never able to explain fully how Hosty's license plate number found its way into Oswald's address book. The reconstruction showed that Oswald's wife, Marina, could not possibly have seen Hosty's car plates on either of his two visits to the Paine house. Hosty never interviewed Lee Harvey Oswald.

35. *Ibid.*, Vol. V, p. 13.

36. *Ibid.*

37. Stern Interview.

38. *Hearings*, Vol. V, pp. 98–119.

39. Rankin Interview II.

40. *Ibid.*

41. *Ibid.*

42. National Archives, *Commission Document* 320.

43. Chronological File, May 21, 1964.

44. *Ibid.*

45. Liebeler Interview.

46. *Ibid.* Also, see note 32 *supra.*

47. Chronological File. Memorandum of May 21, 1964, was returned to Liebeler from Samuel Stern on May 31, with answer "No" to question of whether number was checked in FBI files.

48. Referred to in Hoover testi-

mony, Wade testimony, and Commission Exhibit 833, but never given.

49. *Commission Document* 320,

National Archives (Control Number 767 is withheld).

50. Eisenberg Interview II. Also *Hearings*, Vol. V, p. 12.

3. The Vulnerability of Facts

1. Redlich Interview. Said while maintaining that both men were hit by the same bullet.

2. *Report*, pp. 98–105. The established trajectory, still photographs, and preponderance of eyewitnesses proved Kennedy was not hit before the oak tree.

3. *Hearings*, Vol. IV, pp. 114, 128.

4. *Hearings*, Vol. V, p. 153.

5. *Report*, pp. 193–94, and *Hearings*, Vol. III, p. 407.

6. *Hearings*, Vol. XVII, p. 48.

7. *Report*, Appendix X, pp. 538–543.

8. *Ibid.*, p. 543.

9. *Report*, p. 88.

10. Nate Haseltine, "Kennedy Autopsy Report," *Washington Post*, p. A-3, December 18, 1963. Haseltine told me in an interview that his source was authoritative, and had medical knowledge, and he inferred it came from the White House.

11. E.g., the New York *Herald Tribune*, December 19, 1963, p. 8, stated that the pathologist who performed the autopsy reported "that the first bullet lodged in Kennedy's lung." *The Journal of the A.M.A.* (January 4, 1964, Vol. 187, No. 1, p. 15), said that the first bullet "did not go through the shoulder and was re-

covered during the autopsy." *Newsweek* (December 30, 1963, p. 55) reported: "This bullet, the Navy doctors believe, probably dropped out of the President's body and was the one reportedly found on his stretcher at Parkland."

12. *N.Y. Times*, December 18, 1963, p. 27.

13. *Ibid.*, January 26, 1964, p. 68. "Twelve Unanswered Questions," Jack Langguth.

14. *Hearings*, Vol. V, p. 98.

15. *Ibid.*, p. 98.

16. *Report*, Foreword, p. xi.

17. *Investigation of Assassination of President John F. Kennedy*, p. 18. (Hereinafter FBI Summary Report.) See Appendix A of this book, p. 184.

18. *Ibid.*

19. *Ibid.*, *Supplemental Report, January 13, 1964*, p. 2 (Hereinafter FBI Supplemental Report.) See Appendix B of this book, p. 198.

20. *Report*, p. 88+.

21. *Hearings*, Vol. II, pp. 99, 131.

22. Adams Interview. Adams stated that the FBI had color photographs of the autopsy as well.

23. Specter Interview.

24. *Hearings*, Vol. II, p. 131.

25. *Supra.*

26. The December 9 FBI Summary Report includes an interview

with Marina Oswald conducted on December 3, 1963. See p. 186.

27. *Report*, p. 88.

28. *Ibid.*

29. FBI Summary Report, p. 18. See Appendix A, p. 184.

30. *Report*, p. 88.

31. *Hearings*, Vol. II, p. 350.

32. *Ibid.*, p. 368.

33. According to Francis W. H. Adams, these photographs were in the custody of Attorney General Robert F. Kennedy. Rankin said that they were not introduced into evidence for "reasons of taste."

34. *Ibid.*, Vol. XVII, p. 45.

35. *Ibid.*, Vol. II, p. 143.

36. *Report*, p. 111.

37. *Ibid.*, p. 81 (Kellerman), *Ibid.*, p. 127 (Greer).

38. Photographs were included in Commission Exhibits 393, 394, and 395, but they do not show the bullet holes.

39. *Hearings*, Vol. V, p. 59+.

40. *Ibid.*, p. 60.

41. Interview with Dr. Milton Helpern in Ithaca, N. Y., October 27, 1965 (hereinafter Helpern Interview).

42. *Ibid.*

43. *Ibid.*

44. *Hearings*, Vol. II, p. 93.

45. Helpern Interview.

46. *Hearings*, Vol. II, p. 127.

47. *Ibid.*

48. *Ibid.*, p. 361.

49. *Ibid.*, p. 368.

50. FBI Supplemental Report, pp. 2*ff.* See Appendix B, p. 198.

51. *Report*, p. 88*ff.*

52. *Hearings*, Vol. III, p. 372.

53. *Ibid.*, Vol. VI, p. 5.

54. *Report*, p. 88.

55. *Hearings*, Vol. VI, p. 55.

56. *Report*, p. 50.

57. Helpern Interview.

58. *Hearings*, Vol. V, p. 2+ and Vol. XVIII, Commission Exhibit 833.

4. The Limits of the Investigation

1. Rankin Interview I.

2. Interview with Dr. James Rhodes, Civil Archivist of the National Archives, as well as a limited examination and "spot check" of the investigative reports.

3. *Report*, Foreword, p. xii.

4. Rankin Interview I.

5. *Hearings*, Vol. V, pp. 73–74. Also Vol. II, p. 383.

6. *Report*, p. 249.

7. One witness, James R. Worrell, Jr., testified that he saw an unidentified man run out of the Depository immediately after the shots. *Hearings*,

Volume II, p. 196. Also, Amos Lee Euins said in his testimony that another unidentified witness reported seeing a man run from the building. *Ibid.*, p. 205.

8. *Report*, p. 22.

9. *Ibid.*

10. *Hearings*, Vol. XXIV, p. 522.

11. *Ibid.*

12. *Ibid.*

13. National Archives, *Index of Commission Documents.*

14. *Hearings*, Vol. XV, index, as well as working papers in Liebeler's

files, index of material in *National Archives,* and Specter Interview.

15. For example, two witnesses, Robert E. Edwards and Ronald B. Fisher, among those to see a man in window prior to the assassination, believed originally it was fifth-floor window. *Hearings,* Vol. XIX, pp. 473, 475.

16. *Hearings,* Vol. VI, p. 313 (Harkness).

17. *Hearings,* Vol. VI, pp. 197*ff.* (Fisher), pp. 203*ff.* (Edwards), Vol. XIX, p. 470 (Brennan), Vol. II, p. 171 (Rowland). These were four other witnesses who saw the assassin prior to assassination.

18. *Ibid.,* Vol. II, p. 175.

19. *Report,* p. 252.

20. *Ibid.,* p. 250.

21. Chronological File. Rankin Interviews I and II.

22. Interviews with Willens, Rankin (I and II), Liebeler, and Redlich.

23. *Life,* October 2, 1964, pp. 41*ff.* *N.Y. Times,* September 28, 1964, p. 28 (editorial: "The facts, exhaustively gathered, independently checked and cogently set forth . . . destroy the basis for the conspiracy theories that have grown weedlike in this country and abroad"). *Washington Post,* September 28, 1964, p. A-12 (editorial: ". . . the whole truth and nothing but the truth").

24. The 26 volumes of supporting evidence were not released until November 1964.

25. Goldberg Interview.

26. Rankin Interview I.

27. *Ibid.*

28. *Ibid.*

29. Adams Interview.

30. Willens Interview.

31. *Ibid.*

32. Specter Interview.

33. *Ibid.*

34. *Ibid.*

35. *Ibid.*

36. *Hearings,* Vol. VI, pp. 1–148.

37. The exception is Jean Hill, a witness identified by Mark Lane in his testimony. After his investigation was completed, Specter returned to Dallas to interview Jack Ruby on two occasions.

38. *Report,* p. 90+.

39. *Hearings,* Vol. II, p. 93.

40. *Ibid.,* Vol. II, p. 368.

41. *National Archives,* Commission Documents 5 and 7. Also, Commission Document 3 (the Secret Service Summary Report).

42. *Hearings,* Vol. II, p. 368.

43. *Ibid.,* pp. 368*ff.*

44. *Ibid.,* p. 368.

45. *Hearings,* Vol VI, p. 130.

46. *Ibid.,* p. 131. "*Specter:* And at the time we started our discussion, it was your recollection at that point that the bullet came off stretcher A [Connally's], was it not? *Tomlinson:* B [the other stretcher]. *Specter:* Pardon me, stretcher B, but it was stretcher A you took off the elevator."

47. *Ibid.,* pp. 131*ff.*

48. Specter Interview.

49. *Report,* p. 81.

50. *Hearings,* Vol. VI, pp. 138, 142.

51. *Ibid.*

52. *Ibid.,* Vol. II, p. 382.

53. *Report,* p. 19 (conclusion e-2).

54. *Hearings,* Vol. II, pp. 375–76 (Humes), Vol. IV, p. 113 (Shaw), Vol. IV, p. 127 (Gregory).

55. *Ibid.,* Vol. XXIV, p. 412.

56. *Ibid.,* Vol. VI, pp. 138–43.

57. Specter was in Dallas March 17–25, also on May 23–24, during the period from March 14 to June 1 (investigation).

58. Specter Interview.

59. *Report*, p. 116.

60. *Hearings*, Vol. XXIII, p. 915. (Radio Log: "Patrolman L. L. Hill: 'I have one guy who was possibly hit by a ricochet from the bullet off the concrete.'")

61. Specter Interview, Willens Interview.

62. *Hearings*, Vol. XXIV, p. 540.

63. Ball Interview.

64. Specter Interview.

65. *Hearings*, Vol. XXI, p. 472.

66. Liebeler Interview.

67. *Hearings*, Vol. VII, pp. 553*ff.*

68. *Ibid.*, pp. 544*ff.*

69. *Ibid.*, Vol. XXI, p. 476 (August 12, 1965).

70. *Ibid.*, Vol. XXI, pp. 472*ff.*

71. Liebeler Interview.

72. *Report*, p. 117.

73. Liebeler Interview.

74. Ball Interview.

75. *Ibid.*

76. *Ibid.*

77. *Ibid.*

78. *Ibid.*

79. *Ibid.*

80. *Ibid.*

81. *Report*, pp. 84–85, 118*ff.*

82. Ball Interview, Liebeler Interview.

83. *Report*, p. 249.

84. Liebeler Interview, Chronological File.

85. Ball Interview.

86. *Hearings*, Vol. XXII, p. 833 (Simmons), Vol. VI, p. 225 (Miller), Vol. VI, p. 244 (Holland), Vol. XXII, p. 835 (Murphy), Vol. VI, p. 230 (Reilly), and Vol. VI, p. 251 (Foster).

87. *Hearings*, Vol. XXII, p. 833 (Simmons), Vol. VI, p. 225 (Miller), Vol. XXII, p. 836 (Johnson), and Vol. VI, p. 244 (Holland).

88. *Hearings*, Vol. VI, p. 244.

89. *Hearings*, Vol. XX, p. 843 (J. Newman), Vol. XX, p. 843 (W. Newman), Vol. VII, p. 571 (A. Zapruder), Vol. XIX, p. 486 (A. Millican), Vol. XXIV, p. 525 (J. Chism), Vol. XIX, p. 472 (M. Chism), Vol. XXII, p. 841 (C. Hester), Vol. XXII, p. 841 (M. Hester), Vol. XXIV, p. 520 (M. Woodward).

90. Liebeler Interview.

91. *Hearings*, Vol. XIX, p. 479 (J. Hill), Vol. XIX, p. 467 (H. Betzner), Vol. VII, p. 517 (J. Altgens), Vol. VII, p. 563, (J. Tague), Vol. XXII, p. 846 (J. Franzen), Vol. XIX, p. 487, (M. Moorman), Vol. XXIV, p. 525 (Mrs. Franzen), Vol. XXII, p. 837 (C. F. Brehm).

92. *Hearings*, Vol. II, p. 43, Vol. VI, pp. 205*ff.*

93. *Ibid.*, Vol. VII, pp. 552*ff.*

5. The Limits of the Investigators

1. *Report*, Foreword, p. xiii.

2. *Ibid.*, p. x.

3. Rankin Interview I.

4. *Report*, pp. 479–82 (Staff Biographies).

5. Alfredda Scobey, "A Lawyer's

Notes on the Warren Commission Report," *A.B.A. Journal*, Vol. 51, January 1965, p. 39.

6. Ball Interview.

7. Rankin Interview I.

8. Eisenberg Interview I.

9. Ball Interview.

10. Liebeler Interview.

11. *Hearings*, Vol. II, p. 183.

12. *Ibid.*, p. 184+.

13. *Report*, p. 251.

14. *Ibid.*

15. Liebeler Interview.

16. *Ibid.*

17. Chronological File (September 1, 1964, Memoranum to Willens).

18. Ball Interview.

19. *Hearings*, Vol. V, p. 99.

20. National Archives, Commission Document 1107.

21. E.g., 29 lengthy FBI reports concerned the acquaintances of George Lyman Paine, the father of Michael Paine, with whose wife, Ruth, Marina Oswald was living at the time of the assassination (Commission Documents 600–628).

22. Liebeler Interview.

23. National Archives Index of Investigative Report.

24. Ball Interview, Liebeler Interview. Also, National Archives Index, and all available Secret Service Reports in the National Archives.

25. Rankin Interview I.

26. *Ibid.*

27. *Ibid.*

28. *Ibid.*

29. Liebeler Interview.

30. Ball Interview.

31. Liebeler Interview.

32. *Ibid.*

33. *Ibid.*

34. Chronological File. February 28, 1964, Memorandum: Redlich–Rankin.

35. Liebeler Interview.

36. *Hearings*, Vol. V, p. 607 (and pp. 588*ff.* for other contradictions revealed at this late date).

37. Liebeler Interview.

38. *Hearings*, Vol. V, pp. 255–56.

39. *Ibid.*

40. *Ibid.*, p. 256.

41. *Ibid.*, p. 258.

42. Liebeler Interview.

43. Rankin Interview II.

44. *Report*, p. 813.

45. *Ibid.*, pp. 815–16.

46. Liebeler Interview.

47. *Report*, p. 315.

48. *Ibid.*

49. *Ibid.*, pp. 316–17. Also *Hearings.* Vol. XI, pp. 275*ff.*

50. *Ibid.*, Vol. XI, pp. 275*ff.*

51. Liebeler Interview.

52. *Ibid.*

53. Chronological File. April 3, 1964, Memorandum from Willens.

54. Eisenberg Interview II.

55. Although Congress had given the Commission power to compel testimony from witnesses who claimed the Fifth Amendment (by granting the witnesses immunity), the Commission declined to use this power on several occasions (e.g., Surrey). The reason given by Rankin was that the question of "double jeopardy" (resulting from immunity) was before the courts, and Warren did not want to prejudice his position.

56. Rankin Interview I.

57. McCloy Interview, Dulles Interview.

58. Boggs Interview, Ford Interview, and Cooper Interview.

59. Goldberg Interview.

60. *Report*, pp. 216–21.

61. *Ibid.*, p. 221+.

62. Liebeler Interview.

63. *Report*, p. 219.

64. *Ibid.*, p. 322.

65. Liebeler Interview.

66. *Ibid.*

67. *Ibid.*

68. *Report*, p. 324. "While the FBI had not yet completed its investigation into this matter at the time the report went to press, the Commission had concluded that Lee Harvey Oswald was not at Mrs. Odio's apartment in September of 1963."

6. The Commission Hearings

1. Of the 552 witnesses, 395 were examined by staff lawyers, 61 submitted affidavits, and two witnesses (President and Mrs. Lyndon B. Johnson) submitted unsworn statements.

2. *Hearings*, Vol. I–V.

3. *Hearings*, Vol. II, p. 32, and Vol. V, p. 546 (Mark Lane).

4. *Hearings*, Vol. V, p. 181 (Jack Ruby), and Vol. V, p. 588 (Marina Oswald).

5. Gerald R. Ford, "Piecing Together the Evidence," *Life* magazine, p. 42 (October 2, 1964).

6. *Hearings*, Vol. V, pp. 1–47, 97–129, 213–307, 348–87, 567–88, etc.

7. Eisenberg Interview II.

8. *Hearings*, Vol. II, p. 361 and *passim.*

9. Helpern Interview.

10. *Hearings*, Vol. II, p. 191.

11. Ford Interview.

12. *Hearings*, Vol. II, p. 195+.

13. Report, p. 252.

14. *Supra*, Chapter 5.

15. Ball Interview, Liebeler Interview.

16. Liebeler Interview.

17. Ball Interview.

18. Rankin Interview I.

19. Some of the Commissioners had assistants. Senator Russell requested that Alfredda Scobey, a Georgia lawyer, be appointed to the staff. Gerald Ford had three assistants (John R. Stiles, former Congressman John H. Ray, and Francis X. Fallon, Jr.) to help him in reading and analyzing the record. John J. McCloy had assistance from Patrick Burns, a young lawyer in his office. Senator Cooper, Congressman Boggs, and Allen Dulles stated that they did not have assistants.

20. Rankin Interview II.

21. McCloy Interview.

22. *Ibid.*

23. Rankin Interview II.

24. *Ibid.*

7. The Hypothesis

1. *Report*, Foreword, p. xi.

2. *Ibid.*, pp. 18-20.

3. Redlich Interview.

4. *Ibid.*

5. FBI Summary Report, p. 1. See Appendix A, p. 167.

6. Eisenberg Interview II.

7. *Ibid.*

8. *Hearings*, Vol. V, p. 141.

9. Eisenberg Interview II.

10. Report, p. 98.

11. *Hearings*, Vol. XVII, p. 882.

12. *Ibid.*, Vol. III, p. 407.

13. Eisenberg Interview I.

14. *Hearings*, Vol. V, p. 138.

15. Specter Interview.

16. *Hearings*, Vol. IV, pp. 114, 128.

17. Specter Interview.

18. FBI Summary Report, p. 18. See Appendix A, p. 184.

19. *Hearings*, Vol. II, p. 373, and Vol. XVII, p. 48.

20. *Ibid.*, Vol. XVII, p. 48.

21. FBI Supplemental Report, p. 2. See Appendix B, p. 198.

22. *Hearings*, Vol. II, p. 368.

23. *Ibid.*, p. 377.

24. *Ibid.*, p. 368.

25. *Ibid.*, p. 375.

26. Eisenberg Interview I.

27. *Hearings*, Vol. II, p. 368.

28. *Ibid.*

29. *Supra*, Chapter 4.

30. *Hearings*, Vol. II, p. 382.

31. *Supra*, Chapter 4.

32. *Report*, p. 19.

33. *Hearings*, Vol. IV, pp. 135–36.

34. *Ibid.*

35. *Hearings*, Vol. XVIII, p. 724 (Kellerman), Vol. VI, p. 294 (Hargis), *Ibid.*, p. 291 (B. J. Martin), Vol. XVIII, p. 742 (Clinton Hill), Vol. VII, p. 493 (Willis), Vol. VII, pp. 448*ff*. (O'Donnell), *Ibid.*, p. 473 (Powers), Vol. XVIII, p. 762 (Hickey).

36. *Hearings*, Vol. IV, p. 147.

37. *Ibid.*, p. 116.

38. *Ibid.*, pp. 114, 128.

39. Specter Interview.

40. *Hearings*, Vol. II, p. 381.

41. Specter Interview.

42. *Report*, pp. 580–585.

43. *Hearings*, Vol. V, pp. 86–87.

44. *Ibid.*, p. 86.

45. *Ibid.*, pp. 86–87.

46. *Ibid.*, p. 95.

47. *Ibid.*, p. 96.

48. Specter Interview.

49. *Ibid.*

50. Rankin Interview II.

51. *Report*, p. 97.

52. *Hearings*, Vol. V, p. 171.

53. *Ibid.*

54. *Ibid.*, p. 172.

55. *Ibid.*, pp. 172–73.

56. *Ibid.*

57. Specter Interview.

58. *Ibid.*

59. Liebeler Interview.

60. *Report*, p. 105.

61. *Ibid.* (footnote 292).

62. *Hearings*, Vol. V, p. 174.

63. *Ibid.*

64. *Report*, p. 107.

65. Redlich Interview.

66. *Infra*, Chapter 10.

8. Writing the Report

1. Rankin Interview I.

2. Goldberg Interview.

3. Rankin Interview II.

4. Goldberg Interview.

5. Redlich Interview.

6. *Ibid.*

7. *Ibid.*

8. *Ibid.*

9. Willens Interview.

10. Redlich Interview.

11. Liebeler Interview.

12. Goldberg Interview.

13. *Ibid.*

14. Ball Interview.

15. Liebeler Interview.

16. *Ibid.*

17. Rankin Interview II.

18. *Ibid.*

19. Eisenberg Interview II.

20. *Ibid.*

21. Redlich Interview.

22. *Ibid.*

23. Chronological File, September 8, 1964. The lawyer who wrote it told me that the memorandum was never officially submitted because the deadline was extended from September 11 to September 20.

24. Goldberg Interview.

25. *Ibid.*

26. The first six appendices (33 pages) are procedural documents and information (biographies of Commissioners, List of Witnesses, etc.). Appendix VII, "A Brief History of Presidential Protection," was prepared by Alfred Goldberg and his assistant, Arthur K. Marmor. Appendices VIII and IX are medical documents. Appendix X pertains to expert testimony, and was prepared by Specter, Eisenberg, and Redlich. Appendix XI consists of reports of Oswald's interrogation. Appendix XII deals with "Speculations and Rumors," and was written by Goldberg. Appendix XIII, the longest appendix (72 pages), is a biography of Lee Harvey Oswald, and was written by Lloyd L. Weinreb, then a Department of Justice lawyer temporarily working with the commission. Appendix XIV is an analysis of Oswald's finances prepared by three Internal Revenue Service agents, Philip Barson, Edward A. Conroy, and John J. O'Brien. Appendix XV consists of information concerning Marina Oswald. Appendix XVI is a biography of Jack Ruby written by in part by Laulicht. Appendix XVII is Ruby's polygraph examination written up by Specter. Appendix XVIII consists of reference notes.

9. The Selection Process

1. "A Critique of the Warren Report," *Esquire*, March 1965, p. 61.

2. Redlich Interview.

3. Colloquium (unpublished), July 1964.

4. Willens Interview.

5. Ball Interview.

6. *Ibid.*

7. *Ibid.*

8. *Ibid.*

9. *Ibid.*

10. *Ibid.*

11. Liebeler Interview.

12. *Ibid.*

13. *Ibid.*

14. Chronological File, September 6, 1964.

15. *Report*, p. 168.

16. Ball Interview.

17. *Report*, p. 145.

18. *Ibid.*

19. *Ibid.*

20. Ball Interview.

21. *Report*, p. 144.

22. Ball Interview.

23. *Ibid.*

24. *Report*, p. 143.

25. *Ibid.* p. 145.

26. Ball Interview.

27. *Ibid.*

28. Chronological File, February 28, 1964. See Chapter 5, note 34.

29. Ball Interview.

30. *Ibid.*

31. Redlich Interview.

32. *Ibid.*

33. Liebeler Interview.

34. *Ibid.*

35. Chronological File, September 6, 1964.

36. Liebeler Interview.

37. Chronological File, September 6, 1964.

38. *Report*, p. 128.

39. *Ibid.*, p. 131.

40. Chronological File, September 6, 1964.

41. *Report*, p. 133.

42. *Ibid.*, p. 134.

43. *Ibid.*

44. *Ibid.*

45. Chronological File, September 6, 1964.

46. *Ibid.*

47. *Report*, p. 136.

48. Chronological File, September 6, 1964.

49. *Hearings*, Vol. IV. p. 81.

50. *Ibid.*

51. Chronological File, September 6, 1964.

52. *Hearings*, Vol. IV, p. 87. Eisenberg said, "Now, is it inconsistent with that answer that no fibers were found on the gun which matched the fibers in the blanket?"

53. Chronological File, September 6, 1964.

54. *Ibid.*

55. *Report*, p. 98. The assassin would have had more time if one bullet had hit both the President and Governor Connally, but, as the Commission was unable to decide on whether this happened, the chapter had to show that the assassin had time to fire three separate shots (Redlich Interview).

56. *Hearings*, Vol. III, pp. 403–405.

57. *Ibid.*, p. 404.

58. *Ibid.*

59. *Ibid.*, p. 407.

60. *Ibid.*, p. 405.

61. *Ibid.*, p. 406.

62. *Ibid.*, pp. 441*ff.*

63. *Ibid.*, pp. 446–47.

64. *Ibid.*, p. 444.

65. *Ibid.*, p. 407.

66. *Ibid.*

67. *Ibid.*, p. 444.

68. Chronological File, September 6, 1964.

69. *Ibid.*

70. *Hearings*, Vol. XI, pp. 306*ff*, pp. 301*ff.*

71. *Ibid.*

72. *Ibid.*

73. Chronological File, September 6, 1964.

74. *Ibid.*

75. *Ibid.*

76. *Ibid.*

77. *Report*, p. 191.

78. *Report*, p. 192.

79. Chronological File, September 6, 1964. Also Liebeler Interview.

80. Liebeler Interview.

81. *Hearings*, Vol. VIII, p. 235.

82. *Ibid.*

83. Chronological File, September 6, 1964.

84. *Ibid.*

85. *Ibid.*, March 9, 1964 (Commission Document 434, 451).

86. *Ibid.*

87. Liebeler Interview.

88. *Ibid.*

89. *Ibid.*

90. *Ibid.*

91. *Ibid.*

92. *Ibid.*

93. Rankin Interview II.

94. *Report*, p. 194.

95. *Ibid.*, p. 141, p. 137.

96. *Ibid.*, p. 130.

10. The Commission's Conclusions

1. Ford Interview.

2. *Report*, pp. 18–19.

3. Redlich Interview, Eisenberg Interview II, Specter Interview, Liebeler Interview.

4. *Supra*, Chapter 4. Also, *supra*, Chapters 3 and 7.

5. Ford Interview.

6. Goldberg Interview.

7. Cooper Interview.

8. Boggs Interview.

9. Dulles Interview, McCloy Interview.

10. McCloy Interview.

11. *Ibid.*

12. *Ibid.*

13. *Ibid.*

14. *Report*, p. 19.

15. *Ibid.*, pp. 19–20.

16. *Supra*, Chapter 9.

17. *Ibid.*

18. *Report*, p. 22+.

19. *Ibid.*, p. 23.

20. Liebeler Interview.

21. *Ibid.*

22. Ford Interview.

23. *Hearings*, Vol. V, pp. 607*ff.*

24. Ball Interview.

25. Ford Interview.

26. McCloy Interview.

27. *Report*, p. 22.

28. *Supra*, Chapter 4.

29. *Infra*, Appendices A and B.

30. *Supra*, Chapter 3.

INDEX

221